Aberdeen University Press

List of Manuscripts, Printed Books and Examples of

Bookbinding

Aberdeen University Press

List of Manuscripts, Printed Books and Examples of Bookbinding

ISBN/EAN: 9783337249984

Printed in Europe, USA, Canada, Australia, Japan

Cover: Foto ©Andreas Hilbeck / pixelio.de

More available books at **www.hansebooks.com**

SECOND INTERNATIONAL LIBRARY CONFERENCE

LIST

OF

MANUSCRIPTS, PRINTED BOOKS

AND

EXAMPLES OF BOOKBINDING

EXHIBITED TO THE

AMERICAN LIBRARIANS

ON THE OCCASION OF THEIR VISIT TO HAIGH HALL

ABERDEEN UNIVERSITY PRESS

MDCCCXCVII

LIST OF MANUSCRIPTS, PRINTED BOOKS AND EXAMPLES OF BOOKBINDING.

GREEK MANUSCRIPTS.

1. VITÆ Sanctorum et Martyrum ; Græcé. Folio, on vellum. About A.D. 975.

2. EVANGELIA IV., Græcé, cum Canone Eusebii. Small 4to, on vellum. Sæc. XI.

> Written in a very clear hand, the Canon of Eusebius within elegant borders, illuminated in gold and colours, the heading of each Gospel in letters of gold, within elaborately illuminated ornaments, numerous capitals in gold ; adorned with three large miniatures of St. Matthew, St. Mark, and St. John, executed in colours on a gold ground.

3. EVANGELIA IV., Græcé. Folio, on vellum. About A.D. 1060.

4. EVANGELISTARIUM, Græcé. Folio, on vellum. About A.D. 1060.

5. OFFICIUM ECCLESIASTICUM per totum Annum secundum usum Ecclesiæ Græcæ, Græcé cum notis musicis. Folio, on vellum. Sæc. XI.

6. EVANGELIA IV., Græcé. 8vo, on vellum. About A.D. 1100.

> Written probably by Paul, the Monk, who has inscribed at the end of St. Luke six lines of verse, which appear to be in the same hand as the rest of the book.

7. EVANGELIA IV., Græcé. Sm. 4to, on vellum. About A.D. 1175.

1

8. PSALTERIUM, Græcé.   Sm. 4to, on vellum.   About
A.D. 1200.

9. ST. JOHN DAMASCENE.   Dialectica et Expositio
Fidei Orthodoxæ, Græcé.   4to, on vellum.   Sæc. XII.-XIII.

With numerous diagrams and a full-length drawing of the author.

LATIN MANUSCRIPTS.

10. LEGAL INSTRUMENT OF DONATION FROM JOHAN-
NES, the *Primicerius*, or Captain of a company of soldiers,
to the Church of Ravenna.

> Written on *papyrus*, 5 ft. 4 in. long by 11½ in. broad.   Imperfect at be-
> ginning, and undated; but written probably about A.D. 580—600,
> at Ravenna.
>
> The last portion contained the exact terms of donation, but as the in-
> strument is referred to by the donor just before making his *cross* for
> signature, and by each of the witnesses, it is plain that it was
> meant to be the "*irrevocabilem donationis meæ usufructuariæ
> paginam sex unciarum principalium in integro totius substantiæ
> meæ*".   The language is a very corrupt style of Latin; the hand-
> writing cursive Roman.
>
> One of the most curious features of this document (palæographically
> speaking) is the subscription by one of the witnesses, a Greek,
> Marinos Chrysokatalaktis, who has written his testimony in *Latin*
> but in Greek characters (excepting that he uses the Latin *n*
> for the Greek *v* occasionally, and the Latin *u* for the Greek *β*
> sometimes).   It is a contribution to our knowledge of old Latin
> pronunciation, for we find that he writes ουεικ (that is, *week*, not
> *wyke*) for the Latin *huic*, and that he writes φικετ for *fecit*, in
> which latter word the irregularity of his vowels does not invalidate
> the proof that the letter *c* was still pronounced *k* (not *s*, nor *ch*) at
> the end of the sixth century after Christ.

11. BENEDICTIO CEREI.   Roll, on vellum, 5 ft. 11½ in.
long by 8½ in. broad.   Sæc. IX.

> The blessing of the Paschal candle, a rite beginning with "Exultet,"
> by which word this class of manuscript is frequently called. *The
> illuminations represent the Passion and Resurrection, and the
> music in *neumes* accompany the text.

12. ST. CYPRIAN, Bishop of Carthage. Epistolæ et opuscula. Folio, on vellum, Sæc. VII.-VIII.

> In rude Merovingian characters, often mixed with uncial letters. One of the oldest MSS., still in existence, of this Father of the Church.

13. HOMILIES on the Gospels appointed for the several Saints' days of the year. Small folio, on vellum. About 750-800.

> Written in large rude Carlovingian characters, with a mixture of uncials and capitals. The homilies are by St. Fulgentius, Bede, etc. Belonged originally to the Abbey of Luxeuil.

14. EVANGELIA IV., Latiné, cum Præfatione Beati Hieronymi. Small Fol., on vellum. About 850.

> The illumination prefixed to St. Mark's Gospel is a fine specimen of the Carlovingian art. The writing includes a great variety of characters, uncial, rustic, capital, etc. The numerical figures are according to the Roman system. Initials in gold.

15. EVANGELIA IV., Latiné, cum Canone S. Eusebii. 4to, on vellum. Sæc. IX.

> With illuminations representing the four Evangelists and their symbols, and headings in letters of gold. A note states that the codex was used by St. Anscharius (ob. 865), and was afterwards preserved as a relic in the church at Bremen.

16. S. COLUMBANUS. Vita scripta ab ejusdem discipulo (Jona Hiberno). 4to, on vellum. Sæc. IX.

> Written in the purest Carlovingian character. Some Latin words written with accents like neumes.

17. ST. GREGORY THE GREAT. Moralia in Job. Folio, on vellum. Sæc. IX.

> Written in Spain, and containing numerous glosses. The illuminated capitals are very quaint, being for the most part distorted human figures.

18. SMARAGDUS. Explicationes in Regulam Sancti Benedicti. Folio, on vellum. Sæc. IX.

> Written by a Spanish scribe in visi-gothic letters of a singular form. In three different inks, the body of the work being in black with the headings in red, and the text of the rule in green, or *vice versâ.* Interlaced rustic capitals.

19. EVANGELIA IV., Latiné. 4to, on vellum. Sæc. X.

> Written and illuminated for the Emperor Otto the Great, whose portrait is painted on small medallions with inscriptions round them. The illuminations prefixed to each of the Gospels and the borders of the Canon of Eusebius have been surmised to be by an Italian hand and executed at St. Gallen.

20. LECTIONARIUM. Small 4to, on vellum. About 930.

> With illuminations. Written by Ruoftus, Abbot of Prüm, a monastery on the Moselle, who flourished about the year A.D. 930.

21. EVANGELIA IV., Latiné. 4to, on vellum. Sæc. X.-XI.

> Belonged in the year 1314 to the church of St. Mary, in Walbeck, of which church the " Statuta et Consuetudines " are written on the blank leaves of the volume. With drawings of the Evangelists and initial letters illuminated.

22. BEDA. In Novum Testamentum Tractatus. Folio, on vellum. Sæc. X.-XI.

> Written in double cols., and with many initial letters illuminated. Also miniatures of saints.

23. CANTICA ECCLESIASTICA pro Dominicis et Festis cum Notis musicis. 4to, on vellum. Sæc. X.-XI.

> The music is written without staves, in the notation called *neumes.*

24. JOSEPHUS. Judaicæ antiquitatis libri XX. Belli vero Judaici cum Romanis libri VII. Large folio, on vellum. Sæc. X.-XI.

> In double cols., headings in rustic uncials, and with numerous illuminated capitals, some filling nearly the entire column.

25. BROCARDUS. Magnum Volumen Canonum. Folio, on vellum. Sæc. XI.

With illuminated initials.

26. EPISTOLÆ S. PAULI cum Glossis. Small folio, on vellum. Sæc. XI.

Written in the character used in Europe before the introduction of the angular gothic, with illuminated initials in gold and colours.

27. ST. BERNARD. Sermones de Nativitate Domini, de S. Stephano, etc. Folio, on vellum. Sæc. XI.-XII.

With illuminated initials representing animals in grotesque attitudes.

28. ST. BEATUS (vulgarly called San Biecco, Abbot of Valcavado near Saldano in Castilla la Vieja, died A.D. 798). [Commentarius in Apocalypsim.] At end: Explicit Codex Apocalipsis duodenario ecclesiarum numero ita duodenario ordine librorum incisione distinctio. Incipit explanatio Danielis prophete ab auctore b'i joh'i (S. Hieronymo). In 1 vol., royal folio, on vellum, circa 1150.

With 110 miniatures, all very large, many of them nearly 14 inches by 6 inches in dimension, and some larger still, painted on grounds of deep and vivid colour—including a circular Map of the World. Written in North Spain (Old Castile or Aragon).

29. CASSIODORUS. Expositio digesta Psalmorum. Large folio, on vellum. Sæc. XII.

Written by a Spanish scribe named Cumanxius; with numerous ornamental initials of interlaced work, some of which bear a striking resemblance to the decorative work of the early Celtic School.

30. PSALTERIUM. Folio, on vellum. Sæc. XII.

Written by a German scribe, and ornamented with pen and ink drawings of animals, historiated capitals, and 34 miniatures of the life of Christ in gold and colours.

31. BIBLIA, continens Vetus et Novum Testamentum. 4to, on vellum. Sæc. XIII.

With historiated capitals, etc. Formerly belonged to the Abbey of Saint-Acheul, and to the Duchesse de Berry.

32. BIBLIA LATINA, cum Indice Nominum. Folio, on vellum. Sæc. XIII.

With historiated initials illuminated in gold and colours.

33. BIBLE. The Old and New Testament, illustrated by a series of Miniatures and Extracts. On vellum, in the form of a roll, 30 ft. long, 2 ft. 6 in. wide. About 13th century.

34. MISSALE. Sarum use. Folio, on vellum. About 1228-1256.

Inscribed : " Memoriale Henrici de Cicestria canonici Exoñ. precij. lxs.". Preceding the Canon are eight full-page illuminations, in one of which is introduced a kneeling figure of Canon Henry of Chichester.

35. CHORALE et Hymnarium Ecclesiæ, cum Notis musicis. Large folio, on vellum. Sæc. XIII.

Written in very large missal characters, and adorned with drawings and illuminated capitals. From the Church of Santa Cecilia in Trastevere at Rome.

36. PSALTERIUM. Small folio, on vellum. Written in Paris about A.D. 1260.

With five pages filled with miniatures, and historiated capitals at the commencement of each Psalm. It was probably written by the same person who executed the manuscripts given by St. Louis to the Sainte Chapelle. Belonged at one time to Jeanne de Navarre, Queen Consort of Henry IV., King of England, whose autograph is on one of the blank leaves.

37. PSALTERIUM. Folio, on vellum. Sæc. XIII.

With historiated initials in gold and colours.

38. APOCALYPSE. Historia Sancti Joannis Evangelistæ necnon ejusdem Visiones Apocalypticæ. Small folio, on vellum. Sæc. XIV. (cir. 1350).

> Composed of 24 leaves, containing 96 miniatures, accompanied by explanatory legends, in red or black ink. An admirable production of the Flemish School.

39. SPECULUM humanæ salvationis. Folio, on vellum. Sæc. XIV.

> With rudely painted illuminations.

40. BIBLIA PAUPERUM. Folio, on paper. About A.D. 1400.

> A series of very rude pen and ink drawings illustrating Bible history.

41. VIRGIL. Æneis. Small folio, on vellum. Dated 1404 "de mense Januar. per me B.D.Corsinus".

> Of Italian execution, with the arms of the Corsini family emblazoned at foot of the first page.

42. NICOLAS DE LYRA. Postilla super libros Veteris Testamenti. 3 vols. Folio, on vellum. 1407.

> Presented to a member of the Malatesta family. Italian School; with many illuminations.

43. ARMORIAL GENERAL. Arms and Heraldry. Folio, on vellum. 1416.

> Written by an officer of arms, a native of the Province of Beyra, in Portugal, whilst he was attending the Council of Constance. With 236 coats of arms and flags with heraldic bearings emblazoned.

44. PRECES PRIVATÆ. 4to, on vellum. 1430-1450.

> With many illuminations, executed in Germany about the middle of the 15th century.

45. CASSIANUS. Collationes cum Patribus Egyptiis Habitæ. Super libero Arbitrio Determinatio. De Institutis Patrum et de octo principalibus Vitiis. Folio, on vellum. Sæc. XV.

> Written in Italy, and having the numerous capitals illuminated in gold and colours.

46. PROLIANUS. Compendium Astrologiæ et Astronomiæ. 4to, on vellum. About 1477.

> Written and illuminated by an Italian scribe. The first page is surrounded by an interlaced border, with birds and amorini introduced.

47. PRECES et Officia Varia. Sm. 4to, on vellum, executed at Bruges in 1487.

> Enriched with 30 miniatures and 36 borders, besides other decorations. The artist by whom this volume was decorated with miniatures appears to have been Nicolas de Coutre, one of the Guild of Illuminators of Bruges.

48. HORÆ. Small folio, on vellum. Executed for Jacques Galliot de Gourdon de Genouillac, Grand-Ecuyer de France, and Grand-Maître d'Artillerie under Francis I., 1495-1500.

> Illuminated probably in the South of France by an artist of the school of Jean Foucquet.

49. MISSALE ROMANUM. 6 vols., folio, of which the first and second are exhibited. On vellum. Executed for Cardinal Pompeo Colonna, 1510-17.

> The tradition handed down by the family was that the large full-page illuminations were executed by Raphael, about the year 1517, when the owner was made a cardinal, and there is no doubt that, if not actually by his hand, the work was done by his followers under his supervision.
>
> In all probability we may say that the large miniatures are painted by Timoteo Viti, and the illuminations and arabesques by Litti di Filippo de' Corbizi.

50. HORÆ B. M. Virginis. 32mo (256) ff., on vellum. 16th century.

With illuminations. Belonged to Mary, Queen of Scots, and contains some of her writing on ff. 113 and 124.

51. MICHAEL SCOTT. Magica.—Instructio pro discipulis seu Amatoribus Artis Magicæ. 4to, on vellum. Sæc. XVI.

In Arabic, followed by the Latin translation. Written in red, green and black ink.

52. MS. ON LEATHER. Roll, 32 in. long by 4½ in. wide. Spanish-American. (?) Probably the work of an Indian convert to Christianity, written in peculiar Latin and describing a Local Fight, a Drawing of which is given at the foot. Circa 1500-1530.

53. MS. ON LEATHER. Roll, 36 in. long by 9 in. wide. Spanish-American. (?) An Exercise in Arithmetic in barbarous Latin, with a very strange system of notation. Circa 1500-1530.

54. MS. ON LEATHER. Roll, 10 in. square. Spanish-American. (?) Apparently a Letter or Communication. Circa 1500-1530.

ENGLISH MANUSCRIPTS.

55. YORKSHIRE AND NORTH OF ENGLAND ARMORIAL, called "Stacey Grindle Roll". On vellum. About 1350.

With the arms of sovereigns, nobles and barons emblazoned, and the name and description of each coat written above.

56. GOSPELS IN ENGLISH. The Gospels of the Lord Jhesu Christ, Luk, John, Mathew, Mark. Englished by John de Wycliffe, ãd scribit A.D. 1380. 4to, on vellum.

> This Manuscript was presented to Queen Elizabeth, on her accession to the throne, by Francis Newport, who, for the sake of his religion, had been compelled to fly during the reign of Queen Mary. There is prefixed to it a long letter written by him to the Queen.

57. COOKERY. A Form of Cury, by the Master Cook of Richard the Second. 12mo, on vellum. 1380-1390.

> Black and red ink. 194 receipts. Different from "Pegges Forme of Cury".

58. LYDGATE. Siege of Troy. Folio, on vellum. About 1420.

> With illuminated borders and 70 miniatures. At the beginning is a picture of the author presenting his work to King Henry V. At the end are the arms of William Carent, of Carent's Court, in the Isle of Purbeck, born 1344, and living in 1422, for whom the book was probably written.

59. BOCCACCIO. The Fall of Princes. Translated into English by John Lydgate. Folio, on vellum. About 1425.

> Written in double cols., with borders and capital letters illuminated in gold and colours.

60. ROBERT GLOVER, Somerset Herald. Armorial of English Peers. 4to, on vellum. 1582.

> With 67 coats emblazoned, each of which has a full page, the names and titles being written on the pages facing. Prepared for, and given to, Frederick II., King of Denmark.

61. SIR DAVID LINDSAY II., of the Mount, Lord Lyon King of Arms. Armorial of Scottish Nobles and Barons. Folio, on paper. About 1604.

> With 284 coats of arms emblazoned.

62. MINUTES of Evidence and Actes of Commissioners for the Government of the Borders. Appointed by King James I. Written by Joseph Pennington. Folio, on paper. 1605-6.

63. EDM. SKORY. A Description of all the Islands of the Canaries . . . besides the history of their first inhabitants, called the Guanches. A description of the Islands of Azores. 4to, on paper. About 1610.

> Both works are believed to be unpublished. The first contains the results of Skory's investigations during a residence in the Canaries; the treatise on the Azores is a compilation from other books.

64. JOHN PHILIPOTT, Somerset Herald. Armorial of English Peers. Folio, on vellum. 1635.

> With 66 coats emblazoned, two on each page, the names and titles written above each coat. Prepared for, and given to, Charles Ludovic, Elector Palatine, at the direction of his mother, the Queen of Bohemia.

65. REGICIDES. Volume containing a Collection of Letters and Documents signed by the Judges of King Charles I. and other eminent men of the Commonwealth. Folio, on vellum and paper. 1646-59.

66. JAMES, 7th EARL OF DERBY. Autograph Letter to a Leader of the Rebels refusing to deliver up the Isle of Man. Folio, on paper. Circa 1650.

67. OLIVER CROMWELL. Pass permitting Sir Roger Bradshaigh to proceed freely from London to Haigh. Folio, on paper. 1651.

68. Dr. Samuel Johnson. The Original Round Robin presented to Dr. Johnson, requesting him to write the Epitaph of Goldsmith in English, rather than in Latin. Folio, on paper. 1776.

> Signed by Ed. Gibbon, Jos. Warton, Edm. Burke, Tho. Franklin, A. Chamier, G. Colman, W. Vachell, Sir Joshua Reynolds, Sir W. Forbes, Thomas Barnard, R. B. Sheridan, and P. Metcalfe. One of the signatories, Thos. Barnard, afterwards Bishop of Limerick, was the father-in-law of Lady Anne Lindsay, the writer of " Auld Robin Gray," and it was through her that this interesting document came into the library at Haigh Hall.

69. Lady Anne Barnard. Memoirs. 4to, on paper. 1813-25.

> The volume shown is opened at the place where the authoress has written her celebrated song " Auld Robin Gray ".

70. Lady Anne Barnard. Memoirs. Folio, on paper.

> One of the volumes of the copy which was illustrated with portraits, etc., by the authoress.

FRENCH MANUSCRIPTS.

71. Bible Historiée. 4to, on vellum. About A.D. 1250.

> A series of full-page paintings on a background of burnished gold, representing scenes from the Book of Genesis. The descriptions are written in French above and below the miniatures. Executed in the South of France.

72. Lancelot Del Lac. On reverse of folio 181 : " Mais a tant fenist chi endroit maistre gautiers map son liure de lancelot del lac, si ɔmence a parler du saint graal . . . Chi cōmenche li liures du saint graal". On obverse of 212 : " Chi ɔmenche li liures des mors artus, gauain ꝗ tous les autres ɔpaignons de la taule reonde ꝗ toute la fins". 2 vols. Large folio, on vellum, circa A.D. 1300.

> With 72 interesting miniatures, and numerous illuminated initials.

73. ROMAN DE LA ROSE. 4to, on vellum. 1323.

Written for, and presented to, Christina de Lindesay, Dame de Coucy, shortly after her husband died. A volume of the greatest personal interest to the present owner. Christina de Lindesay was the daughter of Sir William Lindsay, of Lamberton, and his heiress. The house of Lamberton was one of the three branches of the family of Lindsay, founded by the three sons of William de Lindsay, of Crawford, High Justiciary under William the Lion.

74. VIE ET PASSION DE NOSTRE SEIGNEUR JESUS CHRIST. Prières à la Vierge en Rime Française, avec d'autres pièces en prose. Small folio, on vellum. About A.D. 1350.

Written on 53 leaves, of which 24 are ornamented with 26 paintings of Our Lord's Passion, all executed in Grisaille, the aureoles only being depicted with gold, in the style subsequently adopted in the Block Books.

75. JEAN DE COURCY, Chevalier Normand. Chroniques. Large folio, on vellum. A.D. 1420.

With borders and initial letters illuminated in gold and colours.

76. LA RÉGIME DE SANTÉ, fait pour entretenir lomme en bonne disposicion. Folio, on vellum. Sæc. XV.

The first page has an illuminated border and a miniature of the author presenting his book to the patient, and at the foot of the page a coat of arms.

77. PIERRE DESCELIERS, Priest of Arcques. Mappemonde, 8 ft. 2 in. × 4 ft. 1½ in. On vellum. 1546.

Executed by order of Henri II., King of France, at Arcques, near Dieppe, and showing the extent of geographical knowledge in the year 1546. It was formerly in the possession of Jomard, who reproduced it in his *Atlas*.

78. MATHIEU HERBELIN. Généalogie, Épitaphes et Armoiries de tous les Contes et Contesses de Dreux et de Braynne. Folio, on vellum. Sæc. XVI.

With 126 coats of arms emblazoned, and initial letters illuminated in gold and colours.

79. R. P. CHRISTOPHER BUTKENS. Histoire Généalogique de la Maison de Horne. Folio, partly on paper, partly vellum, signed and dated 1630.

> Written by Butkens, and dedicated to Ambrose C^t. de Horne. 118 portraits painted on vellum. All the coats of arms properly emblazoned in metals and tinctures. The manuscript has been continued by another hand to about 1680. It has not been published.

ITALIAN MANUSCRIPTS.

80. PETRARCA. Rime.—Cançoni distese del chiarissimo Poeta Dante Allighieri di Firenze. Folio, on vellum. Sæc. XIV.

> One of the most important manuscripts of the two poets, written during the life-time of Petrarch, or immediately after his death, for Lorenzo, the son of Carlo degli Strozzi (a member of one of the noblest families of Florence), by Paul the Scribe, as appears by the colophon. With large initial letters, and three illuminated borders, containing portraits of the poets and their inamoratas, executed in the finest style of Florentine art at that period, with the arms of the Strozzi emblazoned in the bottom compartment of the first two.

81. DANTE. La Divina Commedia. Folio, on paper. Sæc. XV.

> In double cols. With the Credo and other poems at the end.

82. SAN GIOVANNI CLIMACO. Incōmincia il libro di Sancto Giovanni Climaco della fuga del mondo et della Sancta Scala. Folio, on vellum. Sæc. XV.

> The first page is painted with an allegorical representation of the world, and the means of escape from its perils and follies. A space enclosed within a wall is supposed to represent the world, and here are men and women engaged in its occupations and vanities. In the centre is a painter at his easel, a company of people dance to a tabret and pipe, etc., but one man is seen apparently paying toll to St. Peter. Just outside the gate a woman dons a religious habit, which is handed to her by an angel. A flight of steps leads to the gate of heaven, where a nun is being received by a heavenly spirit. A richly-illuminated border surrounds the whole page, the Heavenly Father in the act of blessing being represented at the top. The binding of this volume is remarkable as an example of the style known as "*cuir bouilli*".

83. MARY, QUEEN OF SCOTS. Narratione del stato della Regina di Scotia . . . nella quele si contengono le persecutioni, travagli et prigionia di essa Regina. . . . 4to, on paper. About 1580.

Manuscript letter from Francesco Marcaldi to his friend Antonio Piacentino.

84. PORTOLANO, including the coasts of Europe, Asia Minor and North Africa. Roll, 3 ft. 6 in. × 2 ft. 9 in., on vellum, 1567.

Ornamented with coloured figures of potentates, representations of cities, and flags with armorial bearings. With inscription "Jacobus maiolus condam vescontis fecit hanc cartam Genue anno domini 1567, die xx Februarij".

85. BOLOGNA. Insegni dei Signori Giudici et Consoli che amministrato Giustizia nella Corte et Tribunale della Universita dei Mercanti della Città di Bologna. Folio, on vellum, 1576-1632.

With 558 coats of arms, besides plan and view of Bologna, and many other paintings by Bernardino Sangiovani.

SPANISH MANUSCRIPT.

86. DIEGO CARCERES. Artezilla dela lengua Otomi. Sm. 4to, on paper. About A.D. 1580.

In gothic handwriting. The first grammar composed in the Otomi language.

CELTIC MANUSCRIPTS.

87. THE ROLL OF FEILIMID—OLAMH NA GAEL. Concerning the early history of the Gaelic Race, the Gael Sciot Iber, extending over a period of about 260 years. On vellum. (?) Sæc. XIV.

88. MATERIA MEDICA. Treatise on Materia Medica—Mineral, Vegetable and Animal. 4to, on vellum. Sæc. XV.

Important as supplying certain lacunæ in a similar MS. in the British Museum.

89. KEATING. History of Ireland. In Irish. Folio, on paper, 1715.

ICELANDIC MANUSCRIPT.

90. RYMBEGLA. Contains : I. A Computistic Treatise dealing with the art of verifying dates. II. A Treatise on Church Ceremonies. III. A Treatise on Physiognomy. IV. A Calendar. V. A Table for showing on what day Easter fell from 1140-1671. 8 × 6 cm., on vellum. About A.D. 1400.

ORIENTAL MANUSCRIPTS.

EGYPTIAN MANUSCRIPTS.

91. SOLAR LITANY, representing the passage of the Sun through one of the hours of the night. 3 ft. 2½ in × 9½ in., on papyrus. About the 20th or 21st dynasty, B.C. 1200-1000.

92. BOOK OF THE DEAD. Portion of the Ritual so called. Roll, in a frame, on papyrus, 21st or 22nd dynasty, B.C. 1100-800. Large vignettes, with text, in cursive hieratic.

93. BOOK OF THE DEAD. Portion of the Ritual so called. Roll, on papyrus, Ptolemaic period, about B.C. 300-100. Vignettes, with text, in hieratic.

COPTIC MANUSCRIPTS.

94. ST. LUKE'S GOSPEL. Fragment in Sahidic or Thebaic, containing ch. iii. 8—vi. 36. Folio, on vellum. Sæc. VI.

95. ST. PAUL'S EPISTLE TO THE GALATIANS. Fragment in Sahidic, containing ch. ii. 8—vi. 16. Folio, on vellum. Sæc. VII.

96. ST. LUKE'S GOSPEL. Fragment in Sahidic or Thebaic, containing ch. xvii. 18—xix. 40. Folio, on vellum. About A.D. 800.

97. FOUR GOSPELS. In Coptic. Folio, on paper. A.D. 1484.

> With rude pictures of the Apostles and of the administration of the Eucharist. An important text in a perfect state of preservation.

SYRIAC MANUSCRIPTS.

98. FOUR GOSPELS. In the original Peshito or "simple" version. 4to, on vellum. About A.D. 550.

> Written in large bold Estranghelo letters of the most archaic character.

99. NEW TESTAMENT. The Gospels of the Peshito version, and the remaining books of the Heraclean version. 4to, on vellum. About A.D. 1000.

> Remarkable as being the only complete Syriac New Testament of any antiquity in any library in Europe. The Apocalypse in the Heraclean version is not found in any other known MS.

100. OCTOËCHUS. Book of the Eight Tones. The Dominical Hymnal and Antiphonal of the Orthodox Syrian Church. Small folio, on paper. A.D. 1456.

> Written in the square so-called Nestorian character, a slight modification of the old Estranghelo.

101. MENÆUM. Offices of the Saints' and other Festival days for the month of August. Folio, on paper. A.D. 1502.

Written in the so-called Nestorian character.

102. OLD TESTAMENT. Portions, comprising Maccabees, Chronicles, Ezra, Nehemiah, Wisdom, Esther, Susanna, Epistles of Jeremiah and Baruch. Folio, on paper. About A.D. 1550.

Written in the Estranghelo characters used by the Nestorians.

103. OLD TESTAMENT. Portions, comprising Isaiah, Jeremiah, Ezekiel, Daniel, Psalms, and some Apocrypha. 4to, on paper. A.D. 1727.

Facsimile of a MS. (probably of the ninth century), which had been carried to China in the time of Chingiz Khân. On Chinese paper, and copied by a Chinese hand.

HEBREW MANUSCRIPTS.

104. NACHMANIDES. Bī 'ūr 'al ha Torah. Cabbalistic Commentary on the Pentateuch. Folio, on vellum. About A.D. 1470-80.

Written in Italy ; with illuminated borders of graceful interlaced work and miniatures.

105. MEGILLAH ESTHER. Scroll of the Book of Esther. Written on 10 skins of vellum. Sæc. xv.

With many curious illustrations and ornamental borders.

106. SEPHER TŌRAH. Scroll of the Law of Moses. Sæc. XV.

Written on many goat-skins in Spain.

107. SEPHER TŌRAH. Scroll of the Law of Moses. Sæc. XV.

Written on many skins of vellum in Germany.

108. SEPHER TŌRAH. Scroll of the Law of Moses. ? Sæc. XVII.

Written on 45 skins of vellum.

SAMARITAN MANUSCRIPTS.

109. PENTATEUCH. 4to, on vellum. A.D. 1211.

Written in bold majuscular characters for public liturgical use.

110. PENTATEUCH. 4to, on vellum, A.D. 1328.

Written in double cols., one containing the Hebrew text and the other an Arabic version.

111. CALENDARIUM SAMARITANUM MAGNUM. Folio, on paper. Sæc. XVIII.

Astronomical Calendar of the Samaritans made to correspond with the Muhammedan Calendar. Besides the Calendar, this MS. contains much that is of the greatest possible interest relating to the Samaritans, *inter alia*, an account of the most ancient Pentateuch preserved at Nablus. The writer gives certain unmistakable indications by which it can be identified.

112. LITURGIA SAMARITANA. Ritual for the Feast of Unleavened Bread. 4to, on paper. Sæc. XVIII.

ARABIC MANUSCRIPTS.

113. AL ḲUR'ĀN. Fragment on vellum, 50 ff., 5 lines to the page, very large Cufic characters. 210 × 295 mm. oblong. About A.D. 750. From Surah 43 v. 15 to 45 v. 5.

114. AL ḲUR'ĀN. Fragment on vellum, 27 ff., in very large Cufic characters. 5 lines to the page. 230 × 320 mm. oblong. About A.D. 750.

115. AL KUR'ĀN. Fragment on vellum, 115 leaves, in Cufic characters, containing Sura 66, v. 11, to Sura 108 (Juz' XXIX. and XXX.), 7 lines to the page. 220 × 130 mm. About A.D. 800.

With gilt ornamentation at the beginning of each Sura. Probably written in Baghdad in the time of Hārūn ar-Rashīd.

116. AL ḲUR'ĀN. Fragment on vellum, 2 ff., small Cufic characters, 11 lines to the page. 127 × 197 mm. oblong. About A.D. 850.

117. AL ḲUR'ĀN. Fragment on vellum, 117 ff., in gold letters, large Cufic characters, 5 lines to the page. 205 × 160 mm. About A.D. 1000.

118. AL ḲUR'ĀN. In later Cufic characters, on Bombycine paper; wanting a few leaves at the end. 235 × 185 mm. About A.D. 1000-1050.

119. FOUR GOSPELS. 265 × 180 mm., on paper. Sæc. XII.

Differs from any of the published editions in very many places.

120. AL ḲUR'ĀN. Fragment containing the 11th Surah and part of the 12th. 370 × 272 mm. 45 ff., beautifully written. About A.D. 1200.

121. AL ḤARĪRI. Al Maqāmāt ul Harīrī. The "Belles Assemblées" of Ḥarīri. Folio, on paper. About A.H. 615-20. A.D. 1218-1223.

Written in the Naskhi character of Baghdād. Remarkable for its age, and the numerous rude but curious illuminations.

122. NEW TESTAMENT. Portions, comprising Acts and the Epistles of St. Paul. 235 × 165 mm., on paper. About A.D. 1250-1300.

An ancient version made from the Syriac Peshito in the 8th century.

123. AL ḲUR'ĀN. 18th Juz'. 230 × 170 mm., on paper. About A.D. 1450.

Written in letters of gold, five lines to the page.

124. ALF LAILA. The Arabian Nights. (Nights, 255-541.) 285 × 200 mm., on paper. About A.D. 1500.

With rude coloured drawings. Probably one of the most ancient ex-tant texts of the book.

125. AL KUR'ĀN. Fragment containing the 2nd Surah, verses 136-253. 305 × 215 mm. In gold letters, 5 lines to the page. About A.D. 1500.

126. AL KUR'ĀN. On Bombycine paper, 467 ff., large Naskhi characters, 10 lines to the page. 860 × 540 mm. About A.D. 1501.

127. AL KUR'ĀN. Transcribed by Mustafa Ibn Nasūh al Lāsiki. 250 × 175 mm. A.H. 910, A.D. 1504.

128. AL KUR'ĀN. 370 × 250 mm., on paper. About A.D. 1525.

With ornamentation of a Persian character.

129. AL KAZWĪNI. 'Ajāïbu l Buldān. The Marvels of (many) Regions. 226 × 135 mm., on paper. A.H. 960, A.D. 1582.

Contains a very curious map showing the world as known to Kazwini, from *Andalus* in the West to Sīn (China) in the East, and from Rūs in the North to the mountains of the Moon in the South.

130. AL FĪRŪZĀBĀDI. Kitābu l Kāmūsi l Muhīt wa l Kābūsi l wasīt. The Embracing Ocean and the Central Model. 310 × 200 mm., on paper. A.H. 1010, A.D. 1601.

A famous lexicon. Elegantly written, with gold ornaments.

131. KALĪLAH WA DIMNAH. Bidpai's Fables. 290 × 200 mm., on paper. A.H. 1083, A.D. 1672.

With rude but spirited drawings.

132. AL BŪṢĪRI. Al Ḳaṣīda Burda. The Poem (named) Burda (the Cloak). 365 × 240 mm. Folded as a screen, on paper. A.H. 1094, A.D. 1682.

Illuminated.

133. AL ḲUR'ĀN. A roll 60 mm. wide, fantastically written. No date, about 1750.

134. AL ḲUR'ĀN. A roll 77 mm. wide, of the same character as the last. No date, about 1750.

135. HĀJI KHALĪFA. Kaŝfu ẓ Ẓunūn 'an asāmi l Kutub wa l Funūn. The Clearing-away of doubts from the names of Books and Sciences. 310 × 190 mm., on paper. A.H. 1170. A.D. 1756.

The revised, corrected, and augmented edition of this well-known bibliographical work, made by Ibrāhīm bin 'Alī Arabatji Baŝi, which was finished the very year of the transcription of this MS.

ETHIOPIC MANUSCRIPTS.

136. ACTS OF ST. GEORGE. 4to, on vellum. About A.D. 1300.

Executed in the best style of Ethiopic calligraphy.

137. ENOCH, Job, IV. Kings. 4to, on vellum. Sæc. XIV.

A Biblical manuscript of unusually early date in this language.

138. ENUMERATION of the Towns which the King of Kings gave to the Holy Michael. Folio, on vellum. Sæc. XVII.

A fragment, with a characteristic illumination of large size.

139. HISTORY OF THE ARCHANGEL MICHAEL. 4to, on vellum. Sæc. XVII.

With illuminations illustrative of the text.

140. PENTATEUCH, Joshua, Judges, Ruth. 4to, on vellum. A.D. 1679.

An important text, as it is written with great care, evidently for use in public worship.

141. FOUR GOSPELS. 4to, on vellum. Sæc. XVIII.

A late, but fine example of calligraphy.

SANSKRIT MANUSCRIPTS.

142. BHĀGAVATA PURĀNA. A roll, 45 ft. 7 in. × 4½ in. About A.D. 1650.

With 48 illuminations. Written in a very minute character.

143. TARKABHÂSHÂBHÂVAPRAKĀŚA. On logic. 64 palm leaves, 18½ in. × 1½ in. About A.D. 1725.

144. DEVA-NĀGARĪ GHĪTA. The Life of Krishna. 16mo, on paper. About A.D. 1775.

With 101 miniatures.

145. BHĀGAVATA PURĀNA. A long roll, on paper. About 1780.

Written in minute characters, and illuminated.

PALI MANUSCRIPT.

146. KAMMAVÂCHÂ. Buddhist Ordination Manual, in Pali. 14 palm leaves, 21 in. × 3¾ in.

Written in the square Pali character, which is not used in writing any other work but the Kammavâchâ.

PANJABI MANUSCRIPT.

147. 'ADI GRANTH. The Religious Code of the Sikhs. Oblong folio, on paper. About A.D. 1650.

Written in the Panjābī language and the Gurumukhī character.

HINDUSTANI MANUSCRIPTS.

148. BHAGAVAT PURĀNĀ. Translated into Hindustani. Sm. folio, on paper. About 1700.

With 146 miniatures of subjects from Indian mythology.

149. RĀG-MALA. Books of the Rāgs. Mythological History of the Origin of the Modes in Music. Folio, on paper. Sæc. XVIII.

With pictures, symbolical and allegorical, which exhibit the life of each musical god with his goddess consort.

150. DJĀNDAK U LŪRK. The Romance of Djandak and his Mistress Lurk. 8vo, on paper. About 1750.

With upwards of 200 miniatures.

MARATHI MANUSCRIPT.

151. ADI PARVA. The First Section of the Sanskrit Epic, the Mahābhārata, in Marathi. Oblong folio, on paper. About A.D. 1780.

With rude drawings.

SINGHALESE MANUSCRIPTS.

152. PANSIYAPANAS-JÂTAKAPOTA. Book of the 550 Birth-stories. The Singhalese Translation of the Pāli Jâtaka-atthakathâ. On 1267 palm leaves. 28 × 2 in.

153. PÛJÂWALIYA. On Buddha's Life and Doctrines. On 436 palm leaves. 21 × 2 in. About 1725.

154. BOOK OF CHARMS. On 10 palm leaves. 10¼ × 2 in.

The leaves sewn together at alternate sides. With curious figures of gods, demons, etc.

155. MAHAVANSA. History of Ceylon. On 38 palm leaves. $14\frac{1}{2} \times 2\frac{1}{2}$ in.

With carved ivory covers.

156-160. INDIAN DRAWINGS. A selection of five volumes of specimens of penmanship and coloured drawings by Indian and Persian artists.

PARSI MANUSCRIPTS.

161. YASNA SÂDAH. The Avesta text of the Yasna or Book of Sacrifice. 8vo, on paper. About A.D. 1725.

Part of the Parsi Scriptures usually called the Zand-avesta.

162. RIVÂYAT-I FÂRSÎ. Persian Rivâyat, or Religious Tradition. 4to, on paper, A.D. 1737-68.

The Rivâyats are replies written or dictated by Irânian priests to questions sent from India. They deal with all the difficult details in the religious practices of the Parsis.

ARMENIAN MANUSCRIPTS.

163. EVANGELIA QUATUOR, Armenicé. 4to, on vellum. Sæc. IX.

A very fine example of the uncial character.

164. ACTS AND EPISTLES. 4to, on vellum. Sæc. XIII.

Written in the Polorkir character of medium size.

165. EVANGELIA QUATUOR, Armenicé. Folio, on paper. A.D. 1313.

With many full-page illuminations probably by a Georgian artist.

166. ALEXANDER THE GREAT. The Marvels of the Life of Alexander of Macedon. 4to, on vellum. 1544.

With illuminations; written in the Polorkir characters of medium size.

167. CHARAGNOTZ. The Book of Charagans or Hymns. 8vo, on vellum. About A.D. 1650.

Written in small Polorkir, with many miniatures, initial letters and other ornaments.

PERSIAN MANUSCRIPTS.

168. KALĪLA WA DIMNA. Fables of Bidpai. 224 × 146 mm., on paper, A.H. 616, A.D. 1219.

Written in Nasxi characters, and is one of the earliest Persian manuscripts in existence.

169. ḤAKĪM SANĀ'Ī OF ƷAZNA. Ḥadīkatu l Ḥaḵīḵat. Garden of Truth. A famous Sūfī poem. 300 × 215 mm., on paper, A.H. 681, A.D. 1282.

Written in bold Nasxi characters, the first three pages illuminated.

170. FIRDAUSI. Šāh-nāma. The Book of Kings. An epic poem on the history of Persia, from the fabulous times to the reign of the last Zoroastrian king Yazdagird. 340 × 220 mm., on paper, A.H. 860, A.D. 1455.

With nineteen miniatures.

171. ANWĀR-I SUHAILI. Splendours of Suhaili (*i.e.*, Canopies). A translation from the Kalīla wa Dimna. 335 × 200 mm., on paper, A.H. 910, A.D. 1504.

With borders of pale gold, worked in figures of birds, beasts, trees and flowers ; also four large miniatures.

172. FIRDAUSI. Šāh-nāma. The Book of Kings. 320 × 190 mm., on paper, A.H. 949, A.D. 1542.

Ruled with gold and decorated throughout. With a large number of miniatures. From the library of the dethroned king of Oude. Probably written in Kashmīr.

173. JĀMI. Yūsuf ū Zulaixā. The Story of Joseph and Zulaikha. 236 × 152 mm., on paper. A.H. 957, A.D. 1550.

With illuminated 'Anwān and miniatures.

174. DĪWĀN OF AMĪR XUSRAU OF DIHLI. 291 × 173 mm., on paper. About A.D. 1550.

With illuminated 'Anwān.

175. FIRDAUSI. Sāh-nāma. The Book of Kings. 313 × 215 mm., on paper. About A.D. 1570.

Written in North India. With nearly 100 miniatures.

176. KULLIYYĀT-I 'URFI. Works of 'Urfi of Shīrāz. 223 × 121 mm., on paper. A.H. 1038, A.D. 1628.

With ornamental borders, illuminated 'Anwāns, and four large miniatures.

177. AL KAZWĪNI. 'Ajā'ibu l Maxlūķāt. The Wonders of Creation. 340 × 183 mm., on paper. A.H. 1041, A.D. 1631.

With 356 miniatures, some of which are very large.

178. KIṢṢA-I HĪR Ū RĀNJAHAN. Tale of Hīr and Rānjahan. 288 × 178 mm., on paper. A.H. 1142. A.D. 1729.

Written within gold lines, and with miniatures.

179. 'IYĀR-I DĀNIŜ. The Touchstone (or Paragon) of Knowledge. A Translation by Abū l Faḍl of the Kalīla wa Dimna. 344 × 225 mm., on paper. A.H. 1212. A.D. 1797.

With miniatures.

180. FIRDAUSI. Sāh-nāma. The Book of Kings. 410 × 250 mm., on paper. A.H. 1227. A.D. 1812.

With a large number of miniatures.

TAMIL MANUSCRIPTS.

181. ARICHANDRAVILÂSAM. Drama which treats of the Trials of Hariśchandra, a Mythical King of Ayodhyá. On 218 palm leaves. 14½ × 1¼ in.

182. BARATHKATHEI. A Condensed Prose Translation of the Mahâbhârata. On 410 leaves. About 1675.

CANARESE MANUSCRIPT.

183. VÂNÎVILÂSA. A Prose Version in Canarese of the Mahâbhârata. By Nanja Râja. 122 palm leaves. 26 in. × 2 in. About A.D. 1700.

Written in the old Canarese character.

TURKISH MANUSCRIPTS.

184. LAILA WA MAJNUN. A Parody of one of Nizami's Poems of the same name by Âmî 'Aî Shîr. 271 × 190 mm., on paper. About A.D. 1475.

With 'Anwān and two miniatures.

185. DRAWINGS OF THE TURKISH SULTANS, and various Officials, Classes, and Craftsmen of the Ottoman Empire. 196 × 143 mm., on paper. About A.D. 1690.

186. RŌZ-NĀMAH. Book of Days. A Perpetual Almanac or Calendar. Roll, 1 m. 45 cm. × 105 mm., on vellum. A.H. 1199, A.D. 1784.

Written in various coloured inks and illuminated.

187. PAGEANT OR PROCESSION OF THE SULTAN. Roll, 9 m. × 295 mm. Sæc. XVIII.

THIBETAN MANUSCRIPTS.

188. TANTRA RAJA. King of Incantations, a Book of Magic. On 130 leaves, black paper, 13 × 4 in.

With the writing in white and yellow paint.

189. ROLL, for Water-wheel, containing a very short formula of Prayer repeated an endless number of times.

190. ROLL, with the same formula in a metal case and handle, for whirling round by hand.

191. MAHĀ-YĀNA SŪTRA. Great-Vehicle Treatise. On 25 leaves, black paper. 13¾ × 4¼ in.

With the writing in yellow paint.

192. NGYEH KRIS. On 35 leaves. 21 × 7 in.

Brown paper, with black ink or paint.

193. SANDALWOOD COVERS for a Thibetan MS., with Mythological Paintings inside the boards.

MONGOLIAN MANUSCRIPTS.

194. ALTAR GEREL. Golden Gleam. Legends of Bodhisatwa. On 166 leaves, paper. 24 × 8 in.

195. SÁNDAN. Daily Prayer to Dshakshimuni. On 9 leaves. 195 × 65 mm.

BURMESE MANUSCRIPTS.

196. TADDHITA-NISSAYA. Nâma-kappam. Treatise on Grammar. Written on 228 palm-leaves. 496 × 54 mm.

197. BURMESE MANUSCRIPT. With Paintings. 402 × 164 mm. On paper, folded like a fan.

198. ASTROLOGICAL and Cabbalistical Treatise. Written in white on black paper. 410 × 160 mm., folded like a fan.

199. FORTUNE-TELLER, and Interpreter of Dreams. 420 × 163 mm., on paper, folded like a screen.
With illustrations.

SIAMESE MANUSCRIPTS.

200. NÁ TON PHRA THAMMA. First page of the August Law. On paper, 437 × 114 mm., folded as a screen. Black on one side and blue on the other.
With many drawings.

201. ASTROLOGICAL CALENDAR, for the Siamese 12 year Cycle. On paper, 365 × 120 mm., folded as a screen.
On white paper, with drawings.

MALAY MANUSCRIPT.

202. MUHAMMADAN PRAYERS and Religious Tracts in Malay. 12mo, on paper. About A.D. 1770.

JAVANESE MANUSCRIPTS.

203. JAVANESE BIBLE STORIES, with paintings illustrative of the text. Folio, on paper. About A.D. 1750.

204. MYTHOLOGY OF JAVA. Drawings in Indian ink of the various Gods and Heroes of the Javanese. Folio, on paper. About A.D. 1800.

205. MYTHOLOGY OF JAVA. Drawings in Indian ink. $13\frac{3}{4} \times 4\frac{7}{8}$ in., on paper, folded as a screen. About A.D. 1800.

206. LEGENDS OF DAMAR WULAN, with coloured drawings. Folio, on paper. About A.D. 1815.

207. HISTORY OF JAVA AND MADURA. Folio, on paper, A.D. 1854.

With twelve pen and ink drawings washed with colour.

BALINESE MANUSCRIPTS.

208. HUSADA. Medicine Book.

Written on the leaves of the Palmyra palm.

209, 210, 211. THREE MANUSCRIPTS of a like appearance to the above, but written in an obsolete character which is almost unknown at Buleleng (or Bliling), the principal town in the island.

BATAK MANUSCRIPTS.

212. PODA. Prescriptions. A Bhatta or Batak Medicine Book.

Written on the bark of a tree, folded as a screen, and apparently very old.

213. PODA. A similar Manuscript containing Prescriptions about various kinds of Witchcraft.

Illustrated with cabbalistic or magical figures.

214. PODA. A similar Manuscript containing Prescriptions about means of Preservation from Evil.

With many magical figures.

BUGI MANUSCRIPT.

215. POEM on the Doctrine of Islam, more especially with regard to the World to come. Folio, on paper. About A.D. 1800.

KAWI MANUSCRIPT.

216. BHARATA YUDDHA. A Fragment of the Kawi Epic Poem. 8vo, on paper. About A.D. 1750.

MADURESE MANUSCRIPT.

217. TANDA ANGRÈK. A Poetic Tale of the Love of Tanda Angrèk for Sarebati. 4to, on paper. About A.D. 1800.

MAKASSAR MANUSCRIPT.

218. POEM in the Makassar language, relating the elopement of a Bugi of the Island of Sambawa with the King's daughter, with their tragic death.

> Three manuscripts written on palm leaves cut to the shape of a ribbon about an inch wide and rolled up. Mounted as wheels on a split bamboo.

CHINESE MANUSCRIPTS AND BOOKS.

219. CHINESE DRAWINGS. Ceremonials and public amusements. On white silk, folded as a screen. Folio.

220, 221, 222. CHINESE DRAWINGS. 3 vols. of paintings representing the history of China. Oblong folio.

223. CHINESE DRAWINGS. Mythological subjects painted on leaves, with the descriptions opposite in gold on a blue ground.

224. CHINESE DRAWINGS. Mythological subjects or folk-lore, painted on silk, 17 × 14 in.

225. CHINESE DRAWINGS. 86 coloured portraits representing different grades and costumes. 14 × 11 in.

226. CHINESE DRAWINGS. Mythological, in pen and ink. 4to.

227. CHINESE DRAWINGS. Trades and costumes of China ; also lepidoptera, flowers, etc. Folio.

228. CHINESE DRAWINGS. Mythological. Highly coloured and mounted on paper. Folio.

229. VIEWS OF REMARKABLE PLACES IN CHINA ; chiefly Mountains. Folded as a screen, 250 × 165 mm.

230. WÊN SHOU CH'Ü KO LO SHANG. Illustrations to a work entitled as above, illustrating the Manners and Customs of the Chinese on one of their great Festivals. 2 rolls, 285 mm. wide.

231. T'IEN CHU CHIANG SHÊNG YEN HSING CHI HSIANG. An Illustrated Life of Christ. By Julio Aleni. 273 × 155 mm. About 1630.

232. INNOCENTIA VICTRIX sive sententia comitiorum Imperii Sinici pro innocentia Christianæ religionis lata juridicé per annum 1669 et jussu R. P. Antonii de Gouvca, S.J. ibidem V. Provincialis Sinico-Latiné exposita. 287 × 180 mm. Quam cheu, 1671.

Printed from wood blocks in the Chinese fashion.

233. VARO. Arte de la lengua Mandarina. 259 × 170 mm. Canton, 1703.

Printed entirely in Roman and italic letter from wood blocks in the Chinese fashion. Only three or four copies known.

234. KUEI CHOU CH'ÜAN SHÊNG PA SHIH ÊRH CHUNG MIAO T'U. Drawings illustrative of the complete Account of the Eighty-two Tribes of the Miao of Kuei-chou. 84 Paintings. 2 vols. Folded as a screen, 305 × 240 mm. About 1750.

235. CHIEH HSIAO SHIH SHIH. The Duties of Chastity and Filial Piety. 310 × 168 mm. 1830.

> Folded as a screen. Printed white on a black ground. With illustrations.

JAPANESE MANUSCRIPTS AND BOOKS.

236. JAPANESE DRAWINGS of Plants, with Descriptions. Folio.

237. RACVYOXV. [Dictionary, so called.] 264 × 190 mm. [Amacusa] In Collegio Japonico Societatis Jesu, 1598.

> Printed from wooden blocks. Of such rarity that only one other copy is known in Europe.

238. RODRIGUEZ. Arte da lingoa de Japam. 4to. Nangasaqui. 1604.

> Printed on Japanese paper. Of such rarity that only one other copy is known.

MEXICAN MANUSCRIPT.

239. DOCUMENT in the Mexican Language, but in European Characters, written upon Maguey paper, or rather felt, constructed from the fibres of the Aloe. 4to. Circa 1530.

EXAMPLES OF BOOK-BINDING IN METAL AND IVORY.

CASE 1.

240. MANUSCRIPT BOOK OF THE EPISTLES.

In the centre of the cover, which is intended to be used as a pax at Mass, is an ivory panel carved in relief with the Crucifixion and figures of the Virgin Mary and St. John the Evangelist. The border is of silver-gilt, decorated with filigree work and four medallions *repoussé*, with figures of Saints; it is further enriched with large crystals, *en cabochon*, and a number of ancient Roman gems and pastes, both in intaglio and cameo. One, cut on red jasper, represents Hermes wearing a chlamys and holding the caduceus, copied from an antique Greek statue resembling the Farnese Hermes in the British Museum: fine Graeco-Roman work of the 1st century, A.D. The ivory carving, German, 10th or 11th century; the border, 13th century.

241. COVERS OF A TEXTUS OR BOOK OF THE GOSPELS.

In the centre of each is an ivory plaque, carved with three subjects in high relief: the Annunciation to the Virgin, the Nativity and Baptism of Christ, the Marys at the Sepulchre, the Ascension of Christ and the Descent of the Holy Ghost. The plaques are mounted in silver-gilt frames, divided into a number of panels, with *repoussé* figures of Our Lord and Saints in high relief, that at the bottom of one being Saint Eucharius, Archbishop of Trèves, where the metal work of this cover was probably made. The intermediate panels are decorated with filigree work, and with jewels and pastes cut *en cabochon*. The ivory carvings, *German*, 10th or 11th century; the frames, 12th century.

242. MANUSCRIPT OF THE OLD TESTAMENT.

In the centre of the cover is an ivory panel carved with two subjects; the upper one represents an archbishop with attendant priests addressing a man seated on a throne; the lower subject represents a Saint about to heal a lame man in the presence of a dignitary seated on a throne. The border, of silver-gilt, is decorated with filigree work and figures in *repoussé*, and enriched with crystals *en cabochon*. The MS. by a German scribe; 11th century; the cover, 13th century.

243. TEXTUS OR BOOK OF THE GOSPELS.

The covers consist of two modern boards in gilt copper frames enriched with plaques of Limoges enamel with representations of Apostles, Virtues, and the symbols of the four Evangelists, and formerly decorated with silver bosses. On one side a metal figure of the Crucifixion was attached, which is now missing; on the other is a 17th century painting of Christ. The MS. *German*, early 12th century.

244. LATIN PSALTER.

The cover is one leaf of the cover of a Textus or Book of the Gospels. In the centre is a figure of the Crucified Christ wearing a jewelled crown, on a cross richly ornamented with coloured enamels; in each corner is an enamelled medallion. The border is enriched with plaques of enamel, filigree work, and jewels. *French (Limoges)*; early 12th century.

245. MANUSCRIPT PRECES ET LECTIONES.

In the centre of the cover is a large shallow depression covered over with thin sheets of gilt copper. Hammered out into low relief are three standing figures—Christ bearing the Book, to the left the Virgin, to the right St. John. Each figure stands on a separate pedestal. Above and below are symbols of the four Evangelists struck on separate pieces of metal of circular shape. The bevel is covered with thin gilt plates. At each corner of the border is a large rock crystal in claw settings; champlevé enamels along the top and bottom, and partly along the sides. The remaining space in the sides are filled with filigree work and jewels. The centre of the cover Byzantine work of the 12th century, the border of a later date. The manuscript of the 15th century.

CASE 2.

246. MANUSCRIPT HORÆ.

The cover, two leaves of an ivory diptych; the front board representing the way to Calvary, and the back board the Crucifixion. Both under a series of Gothic canopies, and with many figures. French work of the 14th century. Manuscript 15th century.

247. Textus or Book of the Gospels.

In the centre of the cover, which is intended to be used as a pax at Mass, is an ivory panel of the Crucifixion, with figures of the Virgin Mary and St. John the Evangelist. The border is of gilt copper engraved with a floriated pattern and studded with silver bosses and jewels; at the corners are Limoges enamel plaques with the four Evangelists. The ivory carving, *Byzantine-German*, 10th or 11th century; the border, early 13th century; the MS., 9th or 10th century, probably written at the Benedictine Monastery of St. Gall, Switzerland. Celtic influence is shown in the illuminated initial letters.

248. Panel.

Ivory, carved in relief, with a figure of Christ delivering the keys to St. Peter with His right hand, and a scroll to St. Paul with His left. The eyes are all jewelled. *Byzantine-German*, 12th century.

249. Manuscript Justinus, Sallustius, Florus.

In the centre of the cover is an ivory representing the Crucifixion. To the left of the cross, the Virgin and St. John, who takes her hand; behind them the holy women in tears; to the right of the cross, two groups of soldiers. Above the cross are two busts of angels. The bevel is covered with hammered metal plates. The border has four large crystals *en cabochon* at the corners, and four enamels *cloisonné* at the sides, top and bottom. The intervening space is occupied by filigree work and jewels. Ivory, 12th century; border, 13th century. The manuscript of the 15th century.

250. Two Leaves of a Diptych.

Ivory, carved in relief with the Annunciation to the Virgin, the Adoration of the Magi, the Nativity of Christ, and the Presentation in the Temple, beneath Gothic arches. *French*, about 1360.

251. Manuscript Latin Psalter.

The binding was probably made for a Textus or a Book of the Gospels. In the centre of one side is a crucifix in gilt and enamelled copper, much worn down with kisses. On the other is a seated figure in gilt copper of Christ holding a book, and with His right hand raised in blessing. *French (Limoges)*, early 12th century. The background is of silver stamped from dies of the 13th century. The whole is surrounded by an ivory border carved with busts of Saints in octagonal panels. ·

252. PANEL.

Ivory, the upper part carved in relief with the Adoration of the Magi, and the lower with the Nativity, it is further decorated with stars and diapers in gold. *German*, 12th century.

253. MANUSCRIPT OFFICIA ET PRECES CONV. NONN. REG. B. SCI AUGUSTINI FLORENTIÆ.

The cover is a metal plate of unusual thickness and weight. It is probably a casting, of which the front surface has been overgilt and chased. The central figure is that of Christ seated on an arch or possibly a rainbow, a serpentine line below may represent the clouds, and between the feet is the globe or earth. To the left and right are embossed the letters A and M, probably to represent Alpha and Omega. In each corner is a rock crystal cut *en cabochon*, and surrounding the principal figure are the symbols of the four Evangelists. At the foot is the Agnus Dei. North Italian, 13th century. The manuscript of the 15th century.

254. MANUSCRIPT HORÆ.

In the centre of the cover an ivory of the Virgin standing, holding on her left arm the Holy Child. Border of gilt copper *repoussé* with turquoises at each corner *en cabochon*, and garnets in the centre of each of the four plates which compose the border. Ivory and border 13th century. Manuscript of the 15th century.

255. MANUSCRIPT BOOK OF THE GOSPELS.

The central recess of the board is covered by a thick plate of copper *champlévé* enamel, on which is nailed a large figure of Christ in benediction, with the book clasped to His breast, seated on a low chair, in very high relief. The figure is of hammered brass or copper, chased and engraved over the surface, and gilt. At the corners of the enamel are the symbols of the four Evangelists. The bevel is covered by a plain strip of gilt metal. The border covered with strips of gilt metal *repoussé*. French (Limoges), early 12th century. The manuscript of the 10th century.

256. COVERS OF A BOOK OF HOURS.

Silver gilt, of a floral design, chased and pierced with plate of the same metal behind. The borders of a wavy pattern. Clasps of similar design as the sides, and treated in like manner. German, 16th century, by W. Jamnitzer.

257. COVERS OF A PONTIFICAL.

Painted on wood ; the front board a full length figure of a Pope with a nimbus and hand raised in benediction on a gold background ; the back board with thirteen coats of arms. The borders of a floral design in gilt and black on a blue ground, with bosses at the corners.

258. PANEL.

Ivory carved in very high relief with a figure of St. James, seated, one hand gathering up his dalmatic and the other clasping an axe and palm leaf against his breast ; background of scroll and leaf design, with inscription S. IACOB⁹. Very grave doubts have been entertained whether this is really a mediæval work of art or not.

259. COVERS OF A BOOK OF THE GOSPELS.

Silver *repoussé* ; the front board a richly jewelled cross, with Christ holding in His left hand an orb, within a circle ; four angels with trumpets at the angles of the cross ; two angels with reaping hook one at each side of the base, that to the right with ears of corn in the hand and a lamb behind ; while the angel to the left holds a bunch of grapes and has a goat behind. The flight into Egypt on the back. The back board is divided into three scenes ; at the top the heavenly choir ; in the centre the Adoration of the Magi ; at the foot St. Joseph and the Shepherds. Armenian, 18th century.

260. CONSULAR DIPTYCH.

Two leaves of carved bone, representing the bust of the Consul Areobindus within a circle, having his monogram above and below. The rest of the design is composed of palm leaves. Both leaves are the same. Roman, early 6th century.

261. COVER OF A TEXTUS OR BOOK OF THE GOSPELS.

Silver plates and border of *repoussé* work on red velvet. In the centre of the front board is the Crucifixion with St. Mary and St. John, and at the four corners cherubs. In the centre of the back board is the Resurrection, and at the four corners the four Evangelists with their symbols. The covers are connected by silver curb chains, four sets of three chains each. Greek or Russian, 16th century.

262. COVERS OF A BOOK OF HOURS,

> Silver gilt, with filigree work of silver and silver gilt representing flowers and leaves, on sides and back. Borders of alternate stars and rectangular pieces surrounded with dots. Clasps of similar design as the sides. Italian, 16th century, by Piero di Nino.

263. COVER FOR A KUR'ĀN.

> A box of silver Damascus work, with a long chain of the same metal for carrying it over the shoulder.

INCUNABULA, ARRANGED CHRONOLOGIC-ALLY UNDER COUNTRIES AND TOWNS.

BLOCK BOOK, etc.

264. SPIEGHEL. Dit is die ploghe vand' spegel onser behoudenisse. Fol. [? 1450].

> The first Dutch edition of the Speculum Block Book.

265. ARS MEMORATIVA. The Bible figured in a series of Rebusses entirely engraved on copper, the plates rudely coloured by hand. The Headings are written in red, and some of the ff. have manuscript explanations. 16mo. Before 1474-5.

> With more than 1200 different subjects.
> On the last folio is written: "Attinet hic Libellus fratr Henrico Haden de Gestrinshausen Ord'is p̄dicator Cōvent Iterensis". This Dominican monastery was closed in 1474-5. Probably unique.

GERMANY—MAINZ.

266. CICERO. Officiorum, lib. iii. ; Paradoxa ; Versus xii. Sapientum. Fol. Mainz, Johann Fust and Peter Schoeffer, 1465.

> The first printed classic, and one of the first two printed books in which Greek characters appear.

267. SAINT JEROME. Epistolæ. 2 vols. Fol. Mainz, Peter Schoeffer, 7th Sept., 1470.

Printed on vellum.

COLOGNE.

268. CICERO. De amicitia et Versus xii. Sapientum. 4to [? Cologne, ? Ulric Zel, ? 1467].

269. CICERO. Synonyma seu de proprietatibus terminorum. 4to [? Cologne, ? Ulric Zel, ? 1467].

270. SENECA. Epistolæ ad Lucillium. Fol. [? Cologne, "R" printer, ? 1470].

271. BREVIARIUM ROMANUM. 4to [? Cologne, ? Johann Koelhoff, ? 1472].

272. G. de SCHUEREN. Vocabularius qui intitulatur Theutonista. Fol. Cologne, Arnold Ter Hoernen, 31st May, 1477.

ELTVIL.

273. VOCABULARIUM Latino-Teutonicum, dictum : Ex quo. 4to. Eltvil, Nicolaus Bechtermuntze, 5th June, 1469. Second edition.

STRASSBURG.

274. VALERIUS MAXIMUS. Facta et Dicta Memorabilia. Folio. [? Strassburg, ? Adolf. Rusch, ? 1469.]

275. ST. ISIDORE. Etymologiarum lib. xx. Folio. [? Strassburg, ? J. Mentelin, ? 1470.]

276. VENERABLE BEDE.   Historia ecclesiastica gentis
Anglorum.   Folio.   [? Strassburg, H. Eggesteyn, ? 1473.]
First edition.

277. SANCIUS   DE   AREVALLO.   Speculum   vitæ
humanæ.   Folio.   [? Strassburg], Martin Flach, 28th
Nov., 1475.

AUGSBURG.

278. PETRUS DE CRESCENTIIS.   Ruralium Commo-
dorum lib. xii.   Folio.   Augsburg, J. Schuszler, 16th
Feb., 1471.   First edition.

279. H. SUSO.   Der Seüsse.   Folio.   Augsburg,
Anthony Sorg, 1482.

ULM.

280. ALBERTUS MAGNUS.   Summa de eucharistiæ
sacramento.   Folio.   Ulm, Johann Zainer, 1474.

281. GUIL. CAOURSIN.   Stabilimenta Rhodiorum Mili-
tum.   Folio.   Ulm, Johann Reger de Kemnat, 23rd Aug.,
1496.

EICHSTÄDT.

282. VOCABULARIUS   Latino-Germanicus.   Folio.
[? Eichstädt, ? Michael Reyser, ? 1475.]

LUBECK.

283. CHRONICORUM   et   historiarum   epitome, rudi-
mentum novitiorum nuncupata.   Folio.   Lubeck, Lucas
Brandis de Schass, 5th Aug., 1475.

284. DAT JUTISCHE LOWBOCK.   4to.   [? Lubeck,
? Stephen Arndes], 1486.

NÜRNBERG.

285. JAC. DE VORAGINE. Legenda sanctorum. Folio.
Nürnberg, Ant. Koburger, 11th Aug., 1478.

286. ANNIUS. Glossa in Apocalypsin, seu liber de
futuris christianorum triumphis contra Saracenos. 4to.
Nürnberg [? Conrad Zeninger, ? 1480].

NETHERLANDS.

287. HORATIUS. Sermones aut Satyræ, libri ii. Folio.
[?   ?   ], 1470.

The earliest dated book with signatures, and the earliest edition of any
part of Horace with a date. The type appears to be Dutch.

UTRECHT.

288. SIDONIUS APOLLINARIS. Opera. Folio. [? Utrecht,
? Ketelær and Leempt, ? 1473.] First edition.

289. VEGETIUS. Epitoma de re Militari. Folio.
[? Utrecht, ? Ketelær and Leempt, ? 1473.] First edition.

HAARLEM.

290. GUIDO DE COLUMNA. Historia destructionis
Trojæ. Folio. [? Haarlem, ?   , ? 1477.]

Dated by the rubricator 1477.

291. OTTO VAN PASSAU. Bœck des gulden throens of
der XXIV. ouden. Folio. Haarlem [? Jacob Bellært],
1484.

DEVENTER.

292. SPECULUM exemplorum ex diversis libris. Folio.
Deventer, Rich. Paffrœt, 2nd May, 1481.

293. PRUDENTIUS. Opera poetica. 4to. [? Deventer, Rich. Paffrœt, ? 1497.]

294. JUVENCUS. Quatuor evangelia hexametris versibus. 4to. [Deventer, Jac. de Breda, ? 1500.]

ANTWERP.

295. CLEM. MAIDSTON. Directorium sacerdotum secundum usum Sarum. 4to. Antwerp, Ger. Leeu, 1488.

ITALY.—SUBIACO.

296. LACTANTIUS. Opera. Folio. Subiaco, [C. Sweynheym and A. Pannartz, 29th Oct., 1465. First edition.

> The first book printed in Italy with a date, and the earliest printed in the Monastery of Subiaco.

297. ST. AUGUSTINE. De Civitate Dei. Folio. [Subiaco, Sweynheym and Pannartz], 1467. First edition.

ROME.

298. LACTANTIUS. Opera. Folio. Rome, Sweynheym and Pannartz, 1468. Second edition.

299. SANCIUS DE AREVALLO. Speculum vitæ humanæ. 4to, Rome, Sweynheym and Pannartz, 1468.

300. ST. AUGUSTINE. De Civitate Dei. Folio. Rome, Sweynheym and Pannartz, 1468. Second edition.

301. ST. JEROME. Epistolæ et Tractatus. 2 vols. Folio. Rome [Sweynheym and Pannartz], 13th December, 1468. First edition.

302. CICERO. De oratore ad Q. fratrem libri iii., etc. 4to. Rome [Sweynheym and Pannartz], 12th January, 1469.

303. APULEIUS. Metamorphoseos libri xi. ac nonnulla alia opuscula. Folio. Rome [Sweynheym and Pannartz], 28th February, 1469. First edition.

304. AULUS GELLIUS. Noctes Atticæ. Folio. Rome, [Sweynheym and Pannartz], 11th April, 1469. First edition.

305. CÆSAR. Opera. Folio. Rome [Sweynheym and Pannartz], 12th May, 1469. First Edition.

306. BESSARION. Adversus calumniatorem Platonis. Folio. Rome, Sweynheym and Pannartz [1469].

307. LIVIUS. Historiarum Romanorum decades III. Folio. Rome, Sweynheym and Pannartz [1469]. First edition.

308. STRABO. Geographia, Latiné. Folio. Rome, Sweynheym and Pannartz [? 1469].
First edition of this version.

309. CICERO. Epistolæ ad familiares. Folio. Rome, Sweynheym and Pannartz, 4th Nov., 1469.

310. LUCANUS. Pharsalia. Folio. Rome, Sweynheym and Pannartz, 1469. First edition.

311. CICERO. Opera philosophica. 4to. [Rome, Ulric Hahn, ? 1469.]

312. PLINIUS SECUNDUS. Historiæ naturalis libri xxxvii. Folio. Rome, Sweynheym and Pannartz, 1470.

313. ST. JEROME. Epistolæ et Tractatus. 2 vols. Folio. Rome, Sweynheym and Pannartz, 1470. Second edition.

314. CICERO. Epistolæ ad M. Brutum, etc. Folio. Rome, Sweynheym and Pannartz, 1470.

315. ST. LEO THE GREAT. Sermones et epistolæ. Folio. Rome, Sweynheym and Pannartz, 1470.

316. LACTANTIUS. Opera. Folio. Rome, Sweynheym and Pannartz, 1470.

Third edition from this press.

317. ST. AUGUSTINE. De Civitate Dei. Folio. Rome, Sweynheym and Pannartz, 1470.

318. QUINTILIANUS. Institutiones oratoriæ. Folio. Rome, Sweynheym and Pannartz [1470].

319. SUETONIUS TRANQUILLUS. Vitæ xii. Cæsarum. Folio. Rome, Sweynheym and Pannartz, 1470.

The first edition from this press.

320. SUETONIUS TRANQUILLUS. Vitæ xii. Cæsarum. Folio. Rome [J. Phil. de Lignamine], Aug., 1470.

First edition, and probably the first book printed by this printer.

321. ST. THOMAS OF AQUINO. Catena aurea. 2 vols. Folio. Rome, Sweynheym and Pannartz, 10th Oct., 7th Dec., 1470.

322. ST. CYPRIAN. Epistolæ et opuscula. Folio. Rome, Sweynheym and Pannartz, 1471. First edition.

323. BIBLIA Latina. 2 vols. Folio. Rome, Sweynheym and Pannartz, 1471.

The first Bible printed in Rome, and probably rarer than the Mazarine Bible.

324. SILIUS ITALICUS. Punicorum libri xvii. Folio. Rome, Sweynheym and Pannartz, 5th April, 1471. First edition.

325. CALPHURNIUS. Eclogæ xi. Hesiodi Opera et Dies. Folio. [Rome, Sweynheym and Pannartz, 1471.]

326. EUTROPIUS. Breviarium historiæ Romanæ. 4to. Rome [George Laver], 20th May, 1471. First edition.

327. CICERO. Orationes. Folio. Rome, Sweynheym and Pannartz, 1471.

With the arms of Diane de Poitiers emblazoned on the first leaf; it has also the stamp of the Royal Library of France.

328. OVIDIUS NASO. Opera. 2 vols. in 3. Folio. Rome, Sweynheym and Pannartz [1471].

329. CICERO. Opera philosophica. 2 vols. Folio. Rome, Sweynheym and Pannartz, 1471.

330. NIC. DE LYRA. Postillæ in Vetus et Novum Testamentum. 5 vols. in 8. Folio. Rome, Sweynheym and Pannartz, 1471-72.

The volume shown contains the celebrated letter to Pope Sixtus IV., giving the catalogue of the works and the number of copies issued by this press. They issued usually 275 copies of each work which they printed.

331. LIVIUS. Historiæ Romanæ decades iii. Folio. Rome, Sweynheym and Pannartz, 16th July, 1472.

332. AULUS GELLIUS.   Noctes Atticæ.   Folio.   Rome
Sweynheym and Pannartz, 6th Aug., 1472.   Second Roman
edition.

333. CÆSAR.   Opera.   Folio.   Rome [Sweynheym
and Pannartz], 25th Aug., 1472.   Second Roman edition.

334. TERENTIUS AFER.   Aelii Donati commentarius
in Terentii comœdias.   Folio.   Rome, Sweynheym and
Pannartz, 10th Dec., 1472.

First dated edition of this commentary.

335. PLINIUS SECUNDUS.   Historiæ naturalis libri
xxxvii.   Folio.   Rome, Sweynheym and Pannartz, 7th
May, 1473.

336. POLYBIUS.   Historiarum libri v. Latiné.   Folio.
Rome, Sweynheym and Pannartz, 31st Dec., 1473.

First edition of this version. The last book printed by the two printers
in partnership before the secession of Sweynheym to work at the
engraving of the maps of the Ptolemy of 1478.

337. XENOPHON.   De Cyri pædia libri viii.   Latiné.
4to.   [Rome, Arnold de Villa, 10th March, 1474.]

First edition of this version.

338. NIC. PEROTTUS.   Rudimenta grammatices.   4to.
Rome, Arnold Pannartz, 2nd Dec., 1474.

The first book printed by Pannartz alone.

339. SENECA.   Epistolæ ad Lucilium libri xxv.   4to.
Rome, A. Pannartz, 1st Feb., 1475.

First edition with a date.

340. HERODOTUS.   Historiarum libri ix. per Laur.
Vallensem e Græco in Latinum conversus.   Folio.   Rome
[A. Pannartz], 20th April, 1475.

341. LAUR. VALLA. De elegantia linguæ Latinæ libri vi. Folio. Rome, A. Pannartz, 2nd July, 1475.

342. TIBULLUS. Elegiarum libri iv. 4to. Rome [? George Laver], 18th July, 1475.

343. STATIUS. Sylvarum libri v. cum Dom. Calderini commentario. 4to. Rome, A. Pannartz, 13th Aug., 1475.

344. HIEROCLES. In aureos versus Pithagoræ opusculum. 8vo. Rome, A. Pannartz, 21st Sept., 1475.

345. SALLUSTIUS. Excerptæ orationes et epistolæ ex libris historiarum. 8vo. Rome, A. Pannartz, 25th Sept., 1475.

346. JOSEPHUS. De bello Judaico libri vii. Folio. Rome, A. Pannartz, 25th Nov., 1475.

347. ST. THOMAS OF AQUINO. Quæstiones disputatæ de veritate. Folio. Rome, A. Pannartz, 20th Jan., 1476.

348. ST. JEROME. Epistolæ et Tractatus. Vol. i. Folio. Rome, Arnold Pannartz, 1476.

> Third edition from the Roman press, and the last production of Pannartz. Laver finished the work by printing the second volume, using the same fount of type.

349. PTOLEMÆUS. Cosmographia. Folio. Rome [C. Sweynheym and] Arnold Buckinck, 10th October, 1478.

> First edition with maps, forming also the first printed atlas, the first book with mathematical figures, and the second printed book with copperplate engravings.

350. PONTIFICALE ROMANUM. Folio. Rome, Stephen Planck, 20th December, 1485.

351. VEGETIUS. Epitome de re militari. 4to. Rome, Eucharius Silber, 29th January, 1487.

4

VENICE.

352. CICERO. Epistolæ ad Atticum, etc. Folio. Venice, Nicholas Jenson, 1470.

353. JUSTINUS. Historiæ ex Trogo Pompeio in epito-men redactæ. 4to. Venice, Nicholas Jenson, 1470. First edition.

354. SALLUSTIUS. Bellum Catilinarium et Jugur-thinum. 4to. Venice, Windelin of Speyer, 1470. Printed on vellum.

355. FLORUS. Epitomatum in T. Livium libri iv. 4to. [? Venice, Francis Renner of Hailbrun, ? 1470.]

356. CICERO. Opera quædam philosophica. 4to. Venice, Windelin of Speyer, 1471.

357. CORNELIUS NEPOS. De vita excellentium virorum. 4to. Venice, Nicholas Jenson, 8th March, 1471. First edition.

358. MARTIALIS. Epigrammata. 4to. [Venice], Windelin of Speyer, [? 1471].

First complete edition.

359. VIRGILIUS MARO. Opera. Folio. [? Venice, ? Windelin of Speyer], 1471.

360. LACTANTIUS. Opera. Folio. [? Venice], Adam [? of Ambergau], 1471.

Printed on vellum.

361. ZOVENZONIUS. Carmen concitatorium in Turcum. 8vo. [? Venice], Adam [? of Ambergau, ? 1471].

362. PLINIUS SECUNDUS. Epistolarum libri viii. 4to. [? Venice, Christ. Valdarfer], 1471. First edition.

363. JOANNES MESUE. Medicinarum universalium liber. Folio. [? Venice, ? Clement of Padua, ? 1471.] First edition.

364. AUSONIUS. Epigrammatum liber et alia opuscula. Folio. Venice, [?], 1472. First edition.

365. CATULLI, Tibulli et Propertii carmina. 4to. [Venice, Windelin of Speyer], 1472. First edition.

This copy belonged to Angelo Politiano, the friend of Lascaris and Lorenzo de Medici. It contains many notes in his handwriting.

366. PRISCIANUS. Opera. Folio. [Venice, Windelin of Speyer], 1472.

First dated edition.

367. SCRIPTORES Rei Rusticæ. Folio. Venice, Nicholas Jenson, 1472. First edition.

368. STATIUS. Thebaidos libri xii. et Achilleidos libri ii. Folio. [? Venice, ? John of Cologne, ? 1472.]

369. SEXTUS RUFFUS. De historia Romana. De ædificationis urbis Venetæ. 4to. [? Venice, Florencius de Argentina, ? 1472.] First edition.

370. CICERO. De legibus. Folio. [? Venice, ? , ? 1472.]

371. DIONYSIUS. Cosmographia seu de situ orbis. 4to. Venice, B. Maler, E. Ratdolt and P. Löslein, 1477.

First edition of this version in prose.

372. ST. JEROME. Vite de sancti padri. Folio. Venice, Nicolao Girardengo, 1479.

373. BARTOLOMMEO DA LI SONETTI.   Isolario in versi. 4to. [? Venice, ?   ? 1480.]

374. EUCLIDES. Elementorum libri xv. Folio. Venice, Erhardt Ratdolt, 25th May, 1482.

First edition of this version, and one of the earliest books in which mathematical figures occur.

375. HOMER.   Batrachomyomachia.   4to.   Venice, Leonicus Cretensis, 22nd April, 1486.

Printed in red and black in alternate lines.

376. MUSÆUS.   Opusculum de Herone et Leandro. 4to. Venice, Aldus Manutius [1494].

First edition, and one of the first productions of the Aldine press.

377. THEO. GAZA.   Introductivæ grammatices libri iv. Folio.   Venice, Aldus Manutius, 25th Dec., 1494.

MILAN.

378. SALLUSTIUS.   Bellum Catilinarium et Jugurthinum.   4to.   [? Milan, ?   ], 1470.

One of the first books printed in Milan.

379. POMPEIUS FESTUS. De significatione verborum. 4to.   Milan [Antonius Zarotus], 3rd Aug., 1471. First edition.

380. THEOCRITUS.   Idyllia xviii., et Hesiodi opera et dies, Græcé.   4to.   [? Milan, ? Dionysius Paravisinus, ? 1480.]   First edition.

381. APOLLONIUS COLLATIUS. De eversione urbis Jerusalem heroicum carmen. 4to. Milan, Ulderic Scinzenzeler and Leon. Pachel, 18th Oct., 1481. First edition.

382. MASUCCIO. Il Nouellino. Folio. Milan, Christopher Valdarfer, 28th May, 1483.

383. APICIUS. De re culinaria. 4to. Milan, Guilernus Signerre, 20th Jan., 1498.
First edition with a date.

384. CICERO. Opera omnia. 4 vols. in 2. Folio. Milan, Alex. Manutianus and the brothers Guielmi, 1498-99. First complete edition.

385. SUIDAS. Lexicon græcum. Folio. Milan, John Bissolus and Benedict Mangius, 15th Nov., 1499.

BOLOGNA.

386. NIC. PEROTTUS. Liber de metris, etc. 8vo. Bologna [? Balthasar degli Azzoguidi], 1471.
One of the earliest books printed in Bologna.

387. VALERIUS FLACCUS. Argonauticon libri viii. Folio. Bologna, Ugo Rugerius and Dominus Bertochus, 7th May, 1474. First edition.

388. MAT. BOSSUS. Recuperationes Fesulanæ. 4to. Bologna, Bazalerus de Bazaleris, 28th Kal. Oct. [sic.], 1493.

VICENZA.

389. VIRGILIUS MARO. Opera. Folio. [? Vicenza] Leonardus Achates, 1472.

390. P. de NATALIBUS. Catalogus sanctorum. Folio. Vicenza, Henricus de Sancto Ursio, 12th Dec., 1493.

BRESCIA.

391. VALERIUS MAXIMUS. Facta et dicta memorabilia. Folio. [? Brescia, ? Thomas Ferrandus, ? 1473.]

392. PROBUS. De litteris antiquis. 4to. [Brescia], Boninus de Boninis, 27th Oct., 1486. First edition.

NAPLES.

393. SENECA. Opera philosophica et epistolæ. Folio. Naples, Mathias Moravus, 1475. First edition.

394. PLINIUS SECUNDUS. Epistolarum libri ix. Folio. Naples, Mathias Moravus, July, 1476.

FLORENCE.

395. CELSUS. De medicina, libri viii. 4to. Florence, Nicolaus Laurentius, 1478. First edition.

396. BERLINGHIERI. Geographia. Folio. Florence, Nicolo Todescho [? 1478].

A rhyming geography with engraved maps.

397. ANTHOLOGIA GRÆCA. Anthologia epigrammatum græcorum Planudis Rhet. Græc. cura J. Lascaris. 4to. Florence, L. F. de Alopa, 11th Aug., 1494.

First edition. Printed throughout in capital letters.

398. GNOMÆ Monostichæ. 4to. [Florence, L. F. de Alopa, ? 1494.]

First edition. Printed in capital letters.

399. APOLLONIUS RHODIUS. Argonauticon cum scholiis græcis. 4to. Florence [L. F. de Alopa], 1496.

First edition. Text printed in capital letters.

400. CALLIMACHUS. Hymni, Græcé, cura J. Lascaris. 4to. [Florence, L. F. de Alopa, ? 1496.]

First edition of the separate Greek text. Printed in capital letters.

401. LUCIANUS SAMOSATENUS. Opera quæ extant omnia. Folio. Florence [? L. F. de Alopa], 1496. First edition.

402. EURIPIDES. Tragœdiæ quatuor : Medea, Hippolytus, Alcestis et Andromache. 4to. [Florence, L. F. de Alopa, ? 1499.]

First edition of the four plays.

403. ORPHEUS. Orphei Argonautica et hymni. Procli Lycii philos. hymni, Græcé. 4to. Florence, Philip Junta, 19th Sept., 1500. First edition.

MANTUA.

404. JOSEPHUS BEN GORION. Historia Judaica, Hebraicé. 4to. [Mantua, ? Abraham Conath, ? 1479.] First edition.

FERRARA.

405. ST. JEROME. Vita e pistole volgare. Folio. Ferrara, Lorenzo di Rossi, 12th Oct., 1497.

FRANCE.—LYONS.

406. DUGUESCLIN. Histoire de Bertrand Du Guesclin. Folio. [? Lyons, ? ? 1480.]

PARIS.

407. LE CHRONIQUE DE FRANCE. 3 vols. Folio. Paris, Jean Maurand for Ant. Verard, 1493.

408. Jean d' Arras. Melusine. Folio. Paris, Pierre Le Caron [? 1495].

409. Merlin. Histoire de la vie de Merlin. Folio. Paris, Ant. Verard, 1498.

410. Le Songe du Vergier. Folio. Paris, Petit Laurens for Jehan Petit [? 1500].

ENGLAND.—LONDON.

411. Chronicle of England. Folio. [London, William de Machlinia, ? 1480.]

412. Speculum Christiani. 4to. London, William de Machlinia [? 1484].

WESTMINSTER.

413. Higden. Polychronicon. Folio. Westminster, William Caxton, 2nd July, 1482.

414. Virgilius Maro. Eneydos. Folio. [Westminster, William Caxton, 1490.]

415. Bart. de Glanvilla. De proprietatibus rerum. Folio. [Westminster, Wynkyn de Worde, ? 1494.]

OXFORD.

416. W. Lyndewood. Constitutiones provinciales ecclesiæ anglicanæ. Folio. [Oxford, Theodoric Rood, ? 1483.]

ST. ALBANS.

417. Chronicles of England, with the Fruit of Times. Folio. St. Albans [?   ? 1484].

SPAIN.—SEVILLE.

418. MOSEN DIEGO DE VALERA. La Cronica de España abreviada. Folio. Seville, Alonzo del Puerto, 1482.

419. JUAN DE MENA. El Labirintho. Folio. Seville, Juan Pegnizer, Thomas and Magnus, 28th Aug., 1499.

TOLEDO.

420. MISSALE MIXTUM, dictum Mozarabes. Folio. Toledo, Peter Hagenbach for Melchior Goricius, 9th Jan., 1500.

421. BREVIARIUM secundum regulas beati Isidori dictum Mozarabes. Folio. Toledo, Peter Hagenbach for Melchior Goricius, 25th Oct., 1502.

BOOKS ON THE LANGUAGES OF NORTH AND SOUTH AMERICA.

422. A. DE MOLINA. Aqui comiença un vocabulario en la lengua Castellana y Mexicana. 4to. Mexico, 4th May, 1555.

423. M. GILBERTI. Arte en la lengua Castellana y en la lengua de Mechoacan. 8vo. Mexico, 1558.

424. M. GILBERTI. Vocabulario en lengua Mechuacan. 4to. [? Mexico], 1559.

425. DOMINGO DE S. THOMAS. Lexicon, o Vocabulario de la lengua general del Peru. 8vo. Valladolid, 1560.

426. A. DE MOLINA.   Vocabulario en lengua Castellana y Mexicana.   Folio.   Mexico, 1571.

427. M. GILBERTI.   Thesoro spiritual de los Pobres en lengua Tarasca.   8vo.   Mexico, 1575.

428. A. VASQUEZ GASTELU.   Arte de lengua Mexicana. 4to.   Puebla de los Angeles, 1589.

429. A. DEL RINCON.   Arte Mexicana.   8vo.   Mexico, 1595.

430. CATECISMO en la lengua Española y Quichua del Peru.   12mo.   Roma, 1603.

431. D. G. HOLGUIN.   Grammatica y arte nueva de la lengua general de todo el Peru, llamada lengua Qquichua. 4to.   Lima, 1607.

432. D. G. HOLGUIN.   Vocabulario de la lengua general de todo el Peru, llamada lengua Qquichua.   4to.   Lima, 1608.

433. L. BERTONIO.   Arte de la lengua Aymara.   8vo. Juli, Chucuyto, 1612.

434. F. DEL CANTO.   Arte y Vocabulario en la lengua general del Peru llamada Quichua, y en la lengua Española. 8vo.   [Lima], 1614.

435. D. DE TORRES RUBIO.   Arte de la lengua aymara. 8vo.   Lima, 1616.

436. B. DE LUGO.   Gramatica en la lengua general del nuevo Reyno, llamada Mosca.   8vo.   Madrid, 1619.

437. A. RUIZ.   Tesoro de la lengua Guarani.   4to. Madrid, 1639.

438. A. RUIZ. Arte, y Bocabulario de la lengua Guarani. 4to. Madrid, 1640.

439. R. WILLIAMS. A Key into the Language of America. 8vo. London, 1643.

440. D. DE REYNOSO. Arte y Vocabulario en lengua Mame. 4to. Mexico, 1644.

441. R. BRETON. Dictionnaire Caraibe-françois. (François-caraibe.) Grammaire caraibe. 3 vols. in 1. 8vo. Auxerre, 1665-67.

442. J. ELIOT. The Indian Grammar begun ; or, an Essay to bring the Indian Language into Rules. 4to. Cambridge, 1666.

443. A. DE VETANCURT. Arte de lengua Mexicana. 4to. Mexico, 1673.

444. F. DE TAUSTE. Arte y Bocabulario de la lengua de los Indios Chaymas, Cumanagotos . . . y otros diversos. de la provincia de Cumana, o Nueva Andalucia. 4to. Madrid, 1680.

445. M. DE YANGUES. Principios y Reglas de la lengua Cummanagota. 4to. Burgos, 1683.

446. GABRIEL DE SAN BUENAVENTURA. Arta de la lengua Maya. 4to. Mexico, 1684.

447. I. MARTENEZ DE ARAUJO. Manual de los Santos Sacramentos en el Idioma de Michuacan. 4to. Mexico, 1690.

448. L. V. MAMIANI. Catecismo da doutrina Christãa na lingua Brasilica da naçao Kiriri. 8vo. Lisboa, 1698.

449. L. V. MAMIANI. Arte de grammatica da lingua Brasilica da naçam Kiriri. 8vo. Lisboa, 1699.

450. N. LOMBARDO. Arte de la lengua Teguima. 4to. Mexico, 1702.

451. P. MARBAN. Arte de la lengua Moxa. 8vo. [Lima, 1702.]

452. BERNARDO DE NANTES. Katecismo Indico da lingua Kariris. 8vo. Lisboa, 1709.

453. D. BASALENQUE. Arte de la lengua Tarasca. 8vo. Mexico, 1714.

454. A. MACHONI DE CERDEÑA. Arte y Vocabulario de la lengua Lule y Tonocote. 8vo. Madrid, 1732.

455. A. DE MOLINA. Doctrina Christina y cathecismo en lengua Mexicana. 4to. Mexico, 1732.

456. B. J. ZAMBRANO. Arte de lengua Totonaca. 4to. La Puebla, 1752.

457. I. J. FLORES. Arte de la lengua metropolitana del reyno Cakchiquel o Guatemalico. 8vo. Guatemala, 1753.

458. C. DE TAPIA ZENTENO. Arte novissima de lengua Mexicana. 4to. Mexico, 1753.

459. J. A. DE ALDAMA Y GUEVARA. Arte de la lengua Mexicana. 16mo. Mexico, 1754.

460. D. DE TORRES RUBIO. Arte, y Vocabulario de la lengua Quichua general de los Indios de el Perú. 8vo. Lima, 1754.

461. G. DE RIPALDA. Catecismo Mexicano que contiene toda la Doctrina Christiana. 8vo. Mexico, 1758.

462. H. CAROCHI. Compendio del Arte de la lengua Mexicana. 4to. Mexico, 1759.

463. A. FEBRES. Arte de la lengua general del reyno de Chile. 8vo. Lima, 1765.

464. L. DE NEVE Y MOLINA. Reglas de orthographia, diccionario y arte del idioma Othomi. 8vo. Mexico, 1767.

465. C. DE TAPIA ZENTENO. Noticia de la lengua Huasteca. 4to. Mexico, 1767.

466. A. DE GUADALUPE RAMIREZ. Breve compendio de todo lo que debe saber, y entender el christiano en lengua Othomi. 4to. Mexico, 1785.

BOOKS OF TRAVEL.

467. DE BRY. Grands et Petits Voyages. 182 vols. Folio. 1590-1644.

This collection of De Bry includes all the parts of all the editions, both in Latin and German, with the single parts issued in English and French, and in addition to these the abridgments and works which are usually added to a set, besides very many varieties of text and plates.

468. THEVENOT. Relations de divers voyages curieux. Folio. Paris, 1663-96.

A copy containing very many variations. Bound in five volumes.

469. GABRIELE CAPODELISTA. Itinerario di Terra Santa, e del Monte Sinai. 4to., without date or place of printing (15th century).

Account of his journey from Venice to Jerusalem, through the Holy Land and Mount Sinai.

470. SCHILDTBERGER.   Ich Schildtberger zoche ausz von meiner heimet mit Namen ausz der stat München gelegen in bayern.   Folio, without date or place of printing (15th century).

> The account of a German soldier named Schildtberger, who was origin- ally a prisoner of Badjazet in Asia Minor.   He was subsequently captured by Tamerlane, and carried into Tartary.   After thirty years' service in his army, he returned to Europe after the death of the great Scythian conqueror.

471. MARCO POLO.   De le meravegliose cose del Mondo. 8vo., Venice, 1496.

472. VESPUCCI.   Paesi nouamente retrouati.   Et nouo mondo da Alberico Vesputio fiorentino intitulato.   4to. Vicenza, 1507.

473. CORSALI.   ¶ Lettera di Andrea Corsali allo illus- trissimo Signo- | re Duca Juliano de Medici, Venuta Dellindia | del Mese di Octobre nel | M.D.XVI. | 4to. Firenze, 1516.

> First edition of Corsali's voyage to India.

474. CORSALI.   Lettera di Andrea Corsali allo Ill. Principe et Signore Lavrentio de Medici Duca Durbino ex India.   [Dated at the end] Ex India quinto decimo Kl. octob. MD.XVII.   8vo.   [? 1518.]

> First edition of Second Letter, describing the return from India.

475. CORTES.   Præclara Ferdinandi Cortesii de Nova maris Oceani Hyspania Narratio. . . . Folio.   Nürnberg, 1524.

> The second and third narratives of Cortes, and the treatise " De rebus et Insulis noviter Repertis ".

476. MARCO POLO. Libro del famoso Marco Polo veneciano. Folio. Logroño, 1529.

477. IL VIAGGIO fatto da gli Spagniuoli a torno a'l Mondo. (Magellan's Expedition.) 4to. 1536.

478. NOVI AVISI di piu l'ochi de l'India et Massime de Brasil ricevuti quest' anno del 1553. 8vo. Rome, 1553.

479. R. EDEN. The History of Travayle in the West and East Indies. 4to. London, 1577.

480. FROBISHER. De M. Forbisseri Navigatione in regiones occidentis et septentrionis narratio historica. 8vo. Nürnberg, 1580.

481. HAKLUYT. The principall Navigations, Voiages and Discoveries of the English Nation, made by Sea or over Land. Folio. London, 1589. First edition.

482. LAUR. KEYMIS. A Relation of the Second Voyage to Guiana. 4to. London, 1596.

483. HAKLUYT. Virginia richly valued, By the description of the maine land of Florida, her next neighbour . . . translated out of Portuguese by R. H. 4to. London, 1609.

484. LESCARBOT. Histoire de la Nouvelle France. 8vo. Paris, 1609.

485. CHAMPLAIN. Les Voyages ou Journal des observations faites és descouvertes de la Nouvelle France. 4to. Paris, 1613.

486. SCHOUTEN. Journal ou description du merveil-
leux voyage fait és années 1615, 1616, & 1617. (Through
the Straits of Magellan to the South Sea.) 4to. Amsterdam, 1618.

487. CHAMPLAIN. Voyages et descouvertes faites en
la Nouvelle France, 1615-1618. 8vo. Paris, 1620.

488. PHILOPONUS. Nova typis transacta Navigatio
Novi Orbis Indiæ Occidentalis. Folio. 1621.

489. RICH. WHITBOURNE. A Discourse and Discovery
of New-found-land. 4to. London, 1622.

490. ALEX. GERALDINUS. Itinerarium ad Regiones
sub Æquinoctiali Plaga constitutas. 8vo. Rome, 1631.

491. GAB. SAGARD THEODAT. Le Grand voyage du
pays des Hurons. 8vo. Paris, 1632.

492. A PUBLICATION of Guiana's Plantation newly
undertaken by the Earle of Barkshire. 4to. London,
1632.

493. HENDRICK BROUWER. Journal van de Reyse
gedaen by Oosten de Straet le Maire, naer de Custen van
Chili in den Jare 1643. 4to. Amsterdam, 1646.

494. PAULMIER. Mémoires touchant l'établissement
d'une mission chrestienne dans le troisième monde. 8vo.
Paris, 1663.

495. LE FEBURE DE LA BARRE. Description de la
France equinoctiale, cy-devant appellée Guyanne. 4to.
Paris, 1666.

496. A RELATION of the Invasion and Conquest of
Florida by the Spaniards. 8vo. London, 1686.

BOOKS NOTED FOR THEIR RARITY OR INTEREST.

497. LUTHER. Disputatio D. Martini Luther Theologi, pro declaratione Virtutis in Indulgentiarum. 4to. [Wittenberg], 1517.

The first and very rare edition of the celebrated Thesis of Luther against the system of Indulgences, which he affixed to the gate of the University of Wittenberg.

498. HECTOR BOECE. Episcoporum Murthlaceñ et Aberdoneñ. Per Hectorem Boetium, Vitæ. 4to. Paris, Ascensianus, 1522.

499. LUTHER. Das tauff buchlin verdeutscht durch Mart. Luther. 4to. Wittenberg, 1523.

First Lutheran baptismal service.

500. LUTHER. Deudsche Messe. 4to. [? Wittenberg], 1526.

In sheets as issued from the press; it has never even been sewed.

501. HUON OF BORDEAUX. Translated by Lord Berners. 4to. [? London, ? Wynkyn de Worde. Circa 1534.]

Believed to be unique.

502. ANNE BOLEYN, QUEEN. Il successo in la Morte della Regina de Inghilterra . . . con le lamentabili parole, que disse la sconsolata Regina in escusatione dil suo peccato. . . . Dated: Di Londra alli X di Giugno 1536. Ser. P.A. 4to. [? Rome, ? 1536.]

Relation by an eyewitness of the execution.

503. HECTOR BOECE. Heir beginnis the hystory and croniklis of Scotland. (On reverse of thirty-sixth preliminary leaf: Heir efter followis the history and croniklis of Scotland compilit and newly correckit be the reuerend and noble clerke maister Hector Boece channon of Aberdene. Translatit laitly be maister Johne Bellenden Archedene of Murray, channon of Ros.) Folio. Edinburgh, Thomas Davidson [? 1542].

504. CHAUCER. Works. Folio. London, 1542.

505. MISSALE ROMANUM. Folio. Venice, 1545.
Printed on vellum, with woodcuts and woodcut borders.

506. W.' PATTEN. The Expedicion into Scotläd of the most woorthely fortunate prince Edward, Duke of Somerset, uncle unto our . . . lord ye kinges Majestie Edward the VI. . . . set out by way of diarie by W. Patten Londoner. . . . 8vo. London, 1548.

507. M. PARKER. De Antiquitate Britannicæ Ecclesiæ. Folio. [London], 1572.
Privately printed. Not more than twenty-five copies are believed to have been issued, and all that are extant differ in their contents. The present copy includes many of the variations.

508. THAME SCHOOL. Schola Thamensis ex Fundatione Johannis Williams Militis Domini Williams de Thame cum Appendicibus. Folio. [London], 1575.
One of the rarest works in English Topography.
In the original oak boards, covered with stamped calf, with brass corners, centres and clasps, having the title of the book printed on vellum, protected by a piece of horn enclosed within brass borders on reverse of cover.

509. JOHN KNOX. History of the Church of Scotland. 8vo. London, 1584.
No complete copy is known. Pages 1-16 and 561 to end were suppressed and destroyed by order of the Archbishop of Canterbury before it was issued in February, 1586.

510. JAMES I. The Essayes of a Prentise in the Divine Art of Poesie. 4to. Edinburgh, 1585. First edition.

511. SPENSER. The Faerie Queene. 2 vols. 4to. London, 1590-96.

First edition of the entire work.

512. H. DYSON. A Booke containing all such Proclamations as were published during the Raigne of Elizabeth (and James I.). Folio. London, 1618.

513. SHAKESPEARE. Mr. William Shakespeare's Comedies, Histories & Tragedies. Published according to the True Originall Copies. Folio. London, 1623.

First folio edition.

514. SHAKESPEARE. Comedies, Histories, and Tragedies. Folio. London, 1632.

Second folio edition.

515. MILTON. Poems, both English and Latin. 8vo. London, 1645. First edition.

516. MILTON. Paradise Lost. 4to. London, 1667.

First edition, with the first title-page.

517. MILTON. Paradise Lost. 4to. London, 1667.

First edition, with the third title-page.

518. MILTON. Paradise Lost. 4to. London, 1667.

First edition, with the fourth title-page.

519. ROBERT HALSTEAD. Succinct Genealogies of the Noble and Ancient Houses of Alno, or de Alneto . . . and Mordaunt of Turvey. Folio. London, 1685.

24 copies printed. Halstead = Pseudonym for Lord Peterborough.

BROADSIDE INDULGENCES.

520. MODUS promerendi indulgentias sacre Crutiate quo ad tres facultates principales. Quarū prima est Iubileus. Folio. [? Mainz, ? Peter Schoeffer, ? 1480-82.]

521. HEREAFT' foloweth the abreuiacōn of the graces, īdulgēces ᵹ staciōs which our moste holy fad' Pope Alexāder vi. graūteth to all true beleuīge people : of euery sexe or kynde wyllīge to enter into the fraternite of the great Hospytall of saynt Iames ī Cōpostell : lately edifyed ᵹ bylded : as is cōteined ī his lett's apostolykes, graūted to euerlastīge memory, ᵹ cōfermed by our holy fad' nowe beīge Pope Iuli⁹. Folio. [? Wynkyn de Worde, ? 1503.]

Probably unique in this impression. Imperfect, only half of the sheet.

522. [BEGINS.] Our holy father pope Leo the .x. that now is cōsiderynge the īfinite charite of our lorde Iesu christe . . . doth exorte all Christē people to charitable warkes : . . . (At the end.) ¶ Abbreuiatio translatiōis bulle Leonis .x. pape moderni, al's translate in vulgare nr̄in, nō de verbo ad verbū, sed quatenus, indulgētias cōtinet, adiectis quibusdā clausulis excerptis a certis trāsumptis autēticis, nihil addito, mutato, aut deleto : qd' alteret, aut mutet effectū prioris translationis facte. Per me walterū Stone legū doctorē. Per me Petrū Potkyn legū Doctorē. Impressum p me Richardū Pynson regiū Impressorē. Folio. London [? 1513-22].

In the top left corner a small woodcut of the Virgin, surrounded by the Apostles, and the Dove descending.

It is a form of Plenary Indulgence to all who contribute to the funds, etc., of the Holy Hospital, but it does not mention where or which the Hospital is, but in all probability that of St. James of Compostella.

523. THE HOLY ꝯ great Indulgence ꝯ pardon of plenary remissiō a pena et culpa graūted by dyuerse popes ꝯ newly confirmed with many amplycacions of our most holy father godes vycar vpō erth pope Leo the .x. that nowe is . . . at the cōmaundemēt of our moost drede soueraygne lorde kyng Henry the .viii. ben examyned by . . . my lord archebysshop of Caunterbury . . . is Institute, publysshed, ꝯ erected in the conuentuall howse of the Graye Freers within the towne of ypswhiche. . . . Oblong 4to. [? Wynkyn de Worde, about 1520.]

> With a rude woodcut of the Descent of the Holy Ghost in the corner.

524. FRATER Johēs Dryuer, Prior Monasterii ordī fratrū sctē crucis in suburbiis Colcestrie . . . Oblong folio. Richard Pynson [1523].

> With rude woodcuts at bottom.
>
> This Indulgence was granted by Leo X. some years before, for the benefit of the Crutched Friars' Monastery, near Colchester. The order was suppressed not long afterwards, and the house became the residence of Sir Harbottle Grimston in the time of the Civil War.

ROYAL PROCLAMATIONS.

ACCESSIONS OF ENGLISH SOVEREIGNS AND CHANGES OF GOVERNMENT.

525. BY THE PRIVY COUNCIL. Death of Queen Elizabeth. 24th March, 1602-3.

526. Declaring that since the Union there is *No* Border. 19th May, 1603.

527. BY THE PRIVY COUNCIL. Death of James I. [25th March], 1625.

528. BY ORMOND, LORD-DEPUTY OF IRELAND. Proclaiming Charles II. to be King of England. 5th Feb., 1648-9.

529. BY O. CROMWELL. Constituting a Council of State to manage the Commonwealth. 30th April, 1653.

530. COUNCIL OF STATE. Declaring Oliver Cromwell to be Lord Protector. 16th Dec., 1653.

531. LORD PROTECTOR. Declaring Oliver, Lord Protector of Commonwealth of England, Scotland and Ireland, to be THE Chief Magistrate. 26th June, 1657.

532. PRIVY COUNCIL. Richard Cromwell proclaimed Protector in place of Oliver, deceased. [3rd Sept.], 1658.

533. Charles II. proclaimed King. 8th May, 1660.

534. BY THE PRIVY COUNCIL. Owing to the death of Charles II., James is proclaimed. [6th Feb.], 1684-5.

535. BY PRIVY COUNCIL OF SCOTLAND. Declaring the death of Charles II., and proclaiming James VII. [6th Feb.], 1684-5.

536. Advice of the intended invasion by Prince of Orange. 28th Sept., 1688.

537. The King, in a Letter to Lord Feversham, Abdicates. 11th Dec., 1688.

538. BY HIS [LATE] MAJESTY. Reasons for withdrawing himself from Rochester. 22nd Dec., 1688.

539. BY THE PRINCE OF ORANGE. For the summoning of a Convention, to be held at Westminster, the 22nd Jan., 1688-9. 29th Dec., 1688.

540. By PARLIAMENT. Proclaiming William and Mary of Orange to be King and Queen of England, etc. 13th Feb., 1688-9.

541. Her Majesty's Declaration at the first Sitting of Her Privy Council. 8th March, 1701-2.

AMERICA.

542. For settling the Plantation of Virginia. 13th May, 1625.

543. Against taking Emigrants or Provisions to New England without License. 1st May, 1638.

544. For Encouragement of Planters in His Majesty's Island of Jamaica. 14th Dec., 1661.

545. Touching the planters in the Island of St. Christophers. 22nd Dec., 1671.

546. By THE PRIVY COUNCIL. Regulations for hiring servants for His Majesty's Plantations in America. 26th March, 1686.

BOOK OF COMMON PRAYER.

547. For Reformation of Church Matters. Bishops to meet. 24th Oct., 1603.

548. Authorising the Book of Common Prayer. 5th March, 1603-4.

549. Confirming the Book of Common Prayer. 16th July, 1604.

BOOKS AND PRINTING.

550. Against import of Latin Books first printed at Oxford or Cambridge. 1st April, 1625.

551. Suppressing two Sermons preached by Dr. R. Mainwaring. 24th June, 1628.

552. Suppressing the book "Appello Cæsarem," by the Bishop of Chichester. 17th Jan., 1628-9.

553. Against importing or buying any foreign edition of "Mare Clausum," the King's book. 15th April, 1636.

554. Against import of Books reprinted beyond seas. 1st May, 1636.

555. Against the book, "An Introduction to a Devout Life," by Nicolas Oakes, and that the same be burnt. 14th May, 1637.

556. Suppressing two books written by John Milton, etc. 13th Aug., 1660.

557. BY THE LORDS. That the "Solemn League & Covenant" be burnt by the Hand of the Common Hangman on the 22nd of May. 20th May, 1661.

558. For reprinting and publishing the book, "God and the King". 5th Dec., 1662.

559. To the Stationers' Company, that nothing be published without the name of the Printer. 22nd Aug., 1679.

560. Against the "Short History of the Convention," a scandalous libel. £100 reward for Author or Printer. 7th May, 1689.

GREAT FIRE OF LONDON.

561. For relief of Sufferers in the Great Fire (2nd, 3rd, 4th Sept.). 5th Sept., 1666.

562. For a proper supply of Provisions to the London Markets. 6th Sept., 1666.

563. BY THE LORD MAYOR OF LONDON. For the rebuilding London. Wren and Hooke to make a Survey. 10th Oct., 1666.

564. BY THE LORD MAYOR. Declaring the names of what are to be known as " Streets of note ". 21st March, 1666-7.

565. BY THE LORD MAYOR. For rebuilding London and widening the principal streets. 29th April, 1667.

GUNPOWDER PLOT.

566. For Apprehension of T. Percy. 5th Nov., 1605.

567. For Apprehension of Catesby, Rookwood, Winter, and others. 7th Nov., 1605.

568. £1000 Reward for Percy. 8th Nov., 1605.

569. For Apprehension of Winter and Littleton. 18th Nov., 1605.

570. Authorising Sheriffs to act outside the boundaries of their own Counties. 19th Nov., 1605

571. For Apprehension of Gerard and others. 15th Jan., 1605-6.

572. To Appease a Rumour of Accident to the King. 22nd March, 1605-6.

POPISH PLOT.

573. For discovery of the Murderers of Sir Edmonbury Godfrey. £500 reward. 20th Oct., 1678.

574. Another on the same subject. 24th Oct., 1678.

575. For a General Fast. (Commencement of " Popish Plot ".) 25th Oct., 1678.

576. £200 Reward for the Murderer of John Powell of London. 22nd Nov., 1678.

577. For further discovery of the Plot. £200 Reward for information. 27th Nov., 1678.

578. For Apprehension of Evars, Gaven, and others (Jesuit traitors). 15th Jan., 1678-9.

RYE HOUSE PLOT.

579. For Apprehension of Colonel Rumsey and others. 23rd June, 1683.

MONMOUTH'S REBELLION.

580. For taking James, Duke of Monmouth, Lord Gray, and others. 28th June, 1683.

581. BY THE PRIVY COUNCIL OF SCOTLAND. For taking James, Duke of Buccleuch (Monmouth). (Edinburgh), 4th July, 1683.

582. Declaring the Duke of Monmouth and Lord Gray to be Traitors. 13th June, 1685.

583. Offering £5000 Reward for the Person of the Duke of Monmouth. 16th June, 1685.

584. Copy of Monmouth's Letter to Lord Albermarle, assuming the title of King. [20th June], 1685.

585. Account of the Taking of the Duke of Monmouth, 8th July. [10th July], 1685.

586. For a Public Thanksgiving for Victory over Rebels (at Sedgemoor). 11th July, 1685.

BIRTH OF PRINCE JAMES ("THE OLD PRETENDER").

587. Public Thanksgiving to be kept for the Queen being with Child (15th and 23rd of Jan.). 23rd Dec., 1687.

588. Thanksgiving for the Birth of a Son to the Queen. 10th June, 1688.

REWARDS OFFERED FOR THE STUART PRINCES.

589. BY THE LORDS JUSTICES OF IRELAND. Against the Duke of Berwick and others by name. £1000 Reward. 11th Nov., 1697.

590. The Pretender (James III.), being about to Invade this country, is declared a Traitor. 6th March, 1707-8.

591. To apprehend James Ogilvie of Boyn, landed from the French Fleet. £300 reward. 22nd March, 1707-8.

592. BY THE PRIVY COUNCIL OF SCOTLAND.   For apprehension of the Person styling himself James III. 25th March, 1708.

593. £5000 reward offered for the Pretender in case he should land.   21st June, 1714.

594. BY THE LORDS JUSTICES OF ENGLAND.   Ordering the payment of £100,000 to any person who shall seize and secure the Pretender in case he shall land, or attempt to land, in any of His Majesty's Dominions.   15th Sept., 1714.

REWARDS OFFERED FOR TRAITORS AND HIGHWAYMEN.

595. £100 reward for Colonel Blood and Lockier, Traitors.   8th Aug., 1667.

596. For Apprehension of certain Robbers (among others, Claude Duval), £20 reward.   19th Nov., 1669.

www.ingramcontent.com/pod-product-compliance
Lightning Source LLC
Chambersburg PA
CBHW031454270326
41930CB00007B/995